The Twelve Steps
A Way Out

The Twelve Steps
A Way Out

A working guide for Adult Children of Alcoholics
and other dysfunctional families

Friends in Recovery

Recovery Publications
1201 Knoxville Street
San Diego, CA 92110
(619) 275-1350

Published by
Recovery Publications
1201 Knoxville Street
San Diego, Ca 92110
(619) 275-1350

The Twelve Steps have been reprinted and adapted with permission from Alcoholics Anonymous World Services, Inc. For purposes of this workbook, the word "alcohol" in Step One has been changed to read "the effects of alcoholism," and the word "alcoholics" in Step Twelve has been changed to read "others."

Printed in the United States of America

Second Printing April 1987
Third Printing July 1987

Recovery Publications

    The Twelve Steps—A Way Out: A working guide for adult children of alcoholics and other dysfunctional families.

1.   2.   1.Title
ISBN   0-941405-03-6 pbk $14.95

In memory of Edward, Cecilia,

and the countless others

who never found "a way out."

In appreciation of the many Adult Children who participated in the experimental Twelve Step Workshops. Their courage and willingness to participate and provide feedback was a vital contribution to this book.

TABLE OF CONTENTS

INTRODUCTION

As Adult Children of alcoholic or dysfunctional families, we have had to face many difficulties in our lives. The behavior patterns we use today are a direct result of our childhood experiences. Having been raised in homes where conditions were chaotic, we did not learn the proper rules needed to function in a normal manner.

Recognition of this often comes slowly. In order to come to terms with the realities of this condition, we must break many of the old family rules, which include not talking, not trusting, and not feeling. Today, these rules keep us from getting in touch with our true selves.

Behavioral problems in Adult Children are numerous, frequently severe, and sometimes incapacitating. Denial is one of the major problems; it keeps us from the reality of our condition. We tend to behave compulsively and always need to be in control. We have not developed the skills needed to express our feelings, so we keep everything locked inside. Our self-esteem is extremely low, and many of us suffer from severe physical complications.

Adult Children suffer from the disease of co-dependency. This is an emotional, psychological, and behavioral condition that develops from prolonged exposure to a set of unspoken and oppressive rules that prevent us from freely expressing our feelings. Co-dependency affects all persons who are in a relationship with an alcoholic, who have alcoholic relatives, or who grew up in an emotionally repressive family.

Being a victim of alcoholic or other dysfunctional behavior causes pain, fear, and inexpressible rage. These feelings cannot be relieved easily. Consequently, we learn to seek relief through superficial means rather than developing normal ways of feeling secure. We experience temporary "highs" through overachievement, overeating, or misuse of mood-altering substances, such as drugs and alcohol. These "highs" manifest themselves in "all-or-none" functioning. In relationships, our behavior may include pursuing someone who is unavailable to us and then distancing ourselves. It may include feeling secure one minute and then suddenly fearing abandonment. Or it may include experiencing sensual pleasure and then an unprompted gut-wrenching fear of rejection. These addictive patterns become a way of life, yet we consider ourselves to be normal.

When we finally come to terms with ourselves, we start looking for answers. After exhausting every effort possible, we finally come to the realization that we cannot do it alone. It is at this point that we are ready to accept help. This help can be found in the Twelve Steps, which is a spiritual program of recovery. It is through this spiritual emphasis that we can begin to experience relief from our problems.

The Twelve Steps is not a religious program. Though people using this program find it harmonious with their churches and spiritual beliefs, it has no religious affiliation. It is, however, a program that helps us to discover the spiritual part of ourselves and recognize its importance in our lives. We learn to live our lives according to the guidance of our Higher Power, whatever that may be. We realize that the void or despair we have felt is caused by ignoring or rejecting the spiritual part of ourselves.

The Twelve Step Program can relieve our suffering, fill our emptiness, and help us discover the presence of a power greater than ourselves. This will help us to release great quantities of energy, love, and joy, which are bottled up inside us. It is a loosely structured program that we follow at our own pace, in our own way, with the help of others who are in the Program. All we need is an open mind and a willingness to try. Eventually, our minds will open by themselves with little conscious effort on our part. Most of the work will be done by our unconscious, and we will suddenly notice improvements in ourselves: our awareness, our sensitivity, our ability to love, to be free. We will be surprised by our own spiritual and emotional growth.

The purpose of this workbook is to help you identify and deal with issues that are interfering with your life. As you work through the problems and rely on the dynamics of the Twelve Steps, you will experience recovery that includes physical, emotional, and spiritual well-being.

Be confident in yourself when completing the work. In this Program, it is important to realize that winners in any field are those who are willing to work and apply themselves in order to succeed. Keeping a positive attitude will be very helpful in your recovery process. Negative thoughts can be very damaging and will slow your progress. Make an effort to surrender to the process, and your negative feelings will be minimized.

Although the focus of this workbook is on the individual, it has been used successfully in groups as a Step Study Writing Workshop. The format of these workshops includes breaking into small "family groups" with a limit of six to seven people per family. These "family groups" work together for a portion of the meeting. The final segment of the meeting involves all "family groups" gathering together for general sharing.

Participants who have attended these workshops have found many benefits and rewards. The experience of being in a small family group creates an atmosphere wherein healthy family communication and interaction can develop. You are encouraged to read Appendix One. The information is intended to help you better understand how maximum benefits can be derived from this workbook, either through self-study or as a participant in a writing workshop. There is no right or wrong way to work the material. Each person has something to contribute in whatever way he or she chooses. The results will vary, but each participant will experience some degree of growth and change.

The Twelve Step material that will be used in this book is meant to be suggestive only. We realize we know very little. As we develop a relationship with our Higher Power, more will be disclosed to us. Ask your Higher Power each day what you can do to take better care of yourself. If you have a good relationship with your Higher Power, your life will become less complicated. Successful completion of this workbook and a commitment to work the Steps as a daily routine for the rest of your life can provide you with the ongoing gift of peace and serenity.

Give freely of what you find and join us. We shall be with you in the Fellowship of Spirit.

GOD BLESS YOU.

The Twelve Steps
A Way Out

NOTICE

IMPORTANT INFORMATION FOR STEP STUDY GROUPS

Appendix One contains methods of study for people participating in a Step Study Writing Workshop. The information is based on the personal experiences of numerous groups who have used the materials.

Appendix Two illustrates specific guidelines and suggestions for starting and conducting a Step Study Writing Workshop. It contains sample meeting formats which are used during the workshop.

Appendix Three contains the weekly exercises which are used during each meeting. These exercises are valuable tools to help the groups in discussing the materials relative to the Step being studied.

STEP ONE

**WE ADMITTED WE WERE POWERLESS OVER THE EFFECTS OF ALCOHOLISM—
THAT OUR LIVES HAD BECOME UNMANAGEABLE**

The idea presented in Step One is overwhelming to most of us until we have begun to see our lives as they really are. It is uncomfortable for us to admit that we are powerless and that our lives are unmanageable. We fight for control and want to keep from being controlled by others. It may be that we are preoccupied with being the smartest or the fastest, or with having the best job. Our obsession may be our status in life, and we find it difficult to believe that we could be powerless. Whatever we do, and however it may be labeled, some of our behavior involves doing things that are against our better judgement. Step One places us on the threshold of identifying the root cause of behavior over which we have no control and which we seem unable to stop.

1. When did you first recognize your need to be in control? _____
   _____
   _____
   _____

2. What happened, and how did you feel? _____
   _____
   _____
   _____

Prior to becoming aware of our problem, we try everything possible to "fix" things. We know that something is wrong and that our life is not working. No matter what we do or where we look, things get progressively worse. We may suffer anxiety attacks, or uncontrollable compulsive behavior. When we actually come to grips with ourselves and realize that we need help, we are ready for Step One. We have no alternative but to admit that we are powerless, and that our lives have become unmanageable.

3. When did you first become concerned about your condition? _____
   _____
   _____
   _____

4. What did you do about it? _____
   _____
   _____
   _____

Step One is the foundation for all the Steps. When working this Step, we see the facts of our lives in true perspective. It is not the purpose of this Step to judge ourselves. It is an opportunity to observe our behavior and to admit that we need help. When we surrender to this idea, we will see our behavior as it really is and be willing to be honest with ourselves. It is through this honesty that we begin to achieve serenity.

5. Describe some of your behaviors that indicate you are operating in a dysfunctional manner and need help. _____

_____

_____

_____

Step One consists of two distinct parts: (1) The admission that we have an obsessive desire to control and that we are experiencing the effects of an addictive process that has rendered us powerless over our own behavior, and (2) The admission that our lives have been, are now, and will continue to be unmanageable by us alone.

6. What difficulties are you having in recognizing your powerlessness? _____

_____

_____

_____

7. What difficulties are you having in recognizing that your life is unmanageable? _____

_____

_____

_____

Admitting our powerlessness over the effects of alcoholism or other addictive behavior is what brings us to the ACA Program. Here we can begin a process of recovery that will transform our lives. Since dysfunctional behavior is a major characteristic of our disease, we must realize that our mind, with its acquired traits, habits, and character defects, has caused us to become powerless over our behavior. By recalling our childhood histories, we see that, years before we realized it, we were out of control. Our obsessions even then were not a habit but indeed the beginning of a fatal progressive disease.

8. What childhood memories most vividly illustrate the fact that you were raised in an unhealthy environment? _____

_____

_____

_____

Our instinct cries out against the idea of personal powerlessness and the fact that we are not in control. We have been accustomed to accepting full responsibility for all that happens in our lives as well as in the lives of others. This contradicts the idea that we are powerless. How can we be fully responsible and at the same time be powerless? Until we hit bottom through utter defeat, we will be unable to take the first step toward liberation and renewed strength. The fact that we are powerless is a truth we must realize before we can totally surrender.

9. What are the major control issues in your life today? _____

_____

_____

_____

10. What is the key issue that caused you to hit bottom and admit utter defeat? _____

_____

_____

_____

Admitting that our lives are unmanageable is equally as difficult as admitting that we are powerless. We see ourselves as responsible adults, holding a job, managing a house, and performing the required tasks on a daily basis. We have been taught from childhood that the best way to succeed is to manage our lives effectively. We were told that truly successful people manage their own lives as well as the lives of others.

11. What is your attitude toward your performance at work or at home? _____

_____

_____

_____

12. How do you see yourself as being unable to manage your life? _____

_____

_____

_____

13. In what area are you having the most difficulty? _____

_____

_____

_____

In order to come to terms with the fact that our lives are unmanageable, we need to recognize that managing our lives is impossible. As we reflect on our lives, we can conclude that no matter what we were doing to manage our lives, the results were never quite what we planned. When we take time to realize that our depressions and frustrations are signs that we are not doing as good a job as we think we are doing, we begin to see the unmanageability. We see how we rationalize our behavior and make excuses for ourselves, blaming our action on fatigue, stress, or other people. Once we can look at our lives objectively and recognize our own faults, we drop our disguise and become more honest with ourselves. We see that our lives are unmanageable and not at all what we would like them to be.

14. Explain situations in which people expressed concern about your behavior. _____

_____

_____

_____

_____

15. Who were they and what caused their concern? _____

_____

_____

_____

Though the First Step may seem overwhelming, it merely points out our human limitations, which have so long been a source of discomfort to us. For most of our lives, we have tried to hide from ourselves. This has prevented us from facing the reality of our situation. Step One is the first step toward the humility we need to find spiritual guidance through reliance on a Higher Power.

16. What are the major limitations that have caused discomfort? _____

_____

_____

_____

17. What does humility mean to you? _____

_____

_____

_____

In the process of accepting our powerlessness and unmanageability, we must be willing to put aside the false pride that nearly killed us. Although working Step One can be painful for us, the road to recovery begins with surrender. Until we accept this truth, our progress toward recovery will be hindered. Although it is difficult for many of us to accept this fact, we must realize that we cannot manage our own lives or control our thinking. Our healing begins when we are willing to acknowledge our problem. This first step forms the foundation for working each of the Twelve Steps.

18. What is the primary behavior pattern or habit you would like to correct in your process of recovery? (e.g., relationship addiction, always having to be right, overpowering guilt, non-assertiveness, fear of abandonment) _____

_____

_____

_____

19. What are the consequences in your life of practicing this behavior pattern or habit? (e.g., violence, unhappiness, feeling out of control, fear of intimacy) _____

_____

_____

_____

_____

20. What is your self-talk (words you say to yourself or thoughts you have) that prompts your behavior? (e.g., He is not going to do this to me again!) _____
_____
_____
_____

21. What is your life rule that prompts your self-talk and subsequent behavior? (e.g., When I grow up, no one is going to push me around. If I don't do it to them first, they will do it to me.) _____
_____
_____
_____

NOTES: _____
_____
_____
_____
_____
_____
_____
_____
_____
_____
_____
_____
_____
_____
_____
_____
_____
_____
_____
_____
_____

THE PROBLEM

The following characteristics are those most commonly found in adult children of alcoholic and other dysfunctional families. They are referred to in the ACA Program as *THE PROBLEM*. The tenses have been changed to reflect the present. The following exercise is intended to help you identify the areas of your life where there are difficulties.

A. **WE ARE ISOLATED AND AFRAID OF AUTHORITY FIGURES.**

1. When did you first become aware that you were isolated and afraid of authority figures? _____

   _____

   _____

   _____

2. In what ways are you experiencing this isolation and fear in your life today? _____

   _____

   _____

   _____

B. **WE ARE APPROVAL SEEKERS AND LOSE OUR IDENTITY IN THE PROCESS.**

1. In what ways did you seek approval from your family or your peers as you were growing up? _____

   _____

   _____

   _____

2. How do you do it today? _____

   _____

   _____

   _____

C. **WE ARE FRIGHTENED BY ANGRY PEOPLE AND ANY PERSONAL CRITICISM.**

1. When do you recall first being frightened by angry people and becoming sensitive to personal criticism? _____

   _____

   _____

   _____

2. How are you dealing with this today? _____

   _____

   _____

D. WE EITHER BECOME ALCOHOLICS, MARRY THEM, OR BOTH—OR WE FIND ANOTHER COMPULSIVE PERSONALITY, SUCH AS A WORKAHOLIC, TO FULFILL OUR NEED FOR ABANDONMENT.

1. Who among your friends, relatives, and business associates demonstrates compulsive personality styles?_____

_____

_____

_____

2. Of your close relationships, describe those who are alcoholic or workaholic, or who manifest other addictive personalities. _____

_____

_____

_____

E. WE LIVE LIFE FROM THE VIEWPOINT OF HELPING AND SEEKING VICTIMS, AND WE ARE ATTRACTED BY THE WEAKNESS IN OUR LOVE AND FRIENDSHIP RELATIONSHIPS.

1. List things you do for others that they could do for themselves so that you feel needed. _____

_____

_____

_____

F. WE HAVE AN OVERDEVELOPED SENSE OF RESPONSIBILITY, AND IT IS EASIER FOR US TO BE CONCERNED WITH OTHERS RATHER THAN WITH OURSELVES. THIS ENABLES US TO AVOID LOOKING CLOSELY AT OURSELVES.

1. Describe those areas of your life in which you feel a high degree of responsibility.

_____

_____

_____

2. Identify those areas you are most concerned about._____

_____

_____

_____

_____

_____

G. **WE FEEL GUILTY WHEN WE STAND UP FOR OURSELVES; INSTEAD, WE GIVE IN TO OTHERS.**

    1.   Identify recent situations in which you were afraid to express your feelings and, instead, gave in to others. _____

_____

_____

_____

H. **WE ARE ADDICTED TO EXCITEMENT.**

    1.   List areas of your life in which you have noticed that you are addicted to the excitement of a relationship, work, or an activity._____

_____

_____

_____

I. **WE CONFUSE LOVE WITH PITY AND TEND TO "LOVE" PEOPLE WE CAN PITY AND RESCUE.**

    1.   Consider the individuals you love. How do you confuse love with pity and tend to love people you can pity and rescue?_____

_____

_____

_____

J. **WE STUFF BACK OUR FEELINGS FROM OUR TRAUMATIC CHILDHOODS AND LOSE THE ABILITY TO FEEL OR TO EXPRESS OUR FEELINGS. IT HURTS SO MUCH—(DENIAL).**

    1.   How do you express your feelings and acknowledge them when something is upsetting you in your work or relationships?_____

_____

_____

_____

K. **WE JUDGE OURSELVES HARSHLY AND HAVE A VERY LOW SENSE OF SELF-ESTEEM, SOMETIMES COMPENSATED FOR BY TRYING TO APPEAR SUPERIOR.**

    1.   In what ways do you think, feel, or act superior in an effort to compensate for your feelings of low self-esteem? _____

_____

_____

_____

L. WE ARE DEPENDENT PERSONALITIES WHO ARE TERRIFIED OF ABANDONMENT. WE WILL DO ANYTHING TO HOLD ON TO A RELATIONSHIP IN ORDER TO AVOID EXPERIENCING THE PAIN OF ABANDONMENT. WE ARE CONDITIONED TO THESE TYPES OF RELATIONSHIPS.

1. When do you experience fear of rejection or abandonment? _____
_____
_____
_____
_____
_____

2. How do you deal with this fear? _____
_____
_____
_____
_____
_____

M. ALCOHOLISM IS A FAMILY DISEASE, AND WE BECOME PARA-ALCOHOLICS. WE TAKE ON THE CHARACTERISTICS OF THAT DISEASE EVEN THOUGH WE DO NOT PICK UP THE DRINK.

1. Having been a victim of an addictive process, in what ways do you manifest the characteristics of co-dependency, alcoholism, eating disorders, obsessive/compulsive thinking and acting? _____
_____
_____
_____
_____
_____

N. PARA-ALCOHOLICS ARE REACTORS RATHER THAN ACTORS.

1. How do you see yourself as a reactor rather than an actor? _____
_____
_____
_____
_____
_____
_____
_____

NOTES: _____

STEP TWO

CAME TO BELIEVE THAT A POWER GREATER THAN OURSELVES COULD RESTORE US TO SANITY

Acceptance of our powerlessness leads us naturally into Step Two. By this time, we have begun to see the results of our past beliefs. "Came to believe" implies a former non-belief, or living life with other beliefs. The result of this lifestyle is our powerlessness and unmanageability. For some of us, belief in our self-will was all we had. Belief in a Higher Power did not seem necessary. Until we took Step One and admitted our powerlessness and unmanageability, we were operating on self-will alone. We simply did not entertain the idea of a Higher Power. As we begin to accept the notion of a Power greater than ourselves, we start to function in a healthier way. We begin to feel a sense of peace and serenity that we had never felt before. We recognize that we are human beings who are struggling to survive with certain limitations.

1. What are some of the fears that block your acceptance of a Higher Power? _____

    _____

    _____

    _____

Step Two is referred to as the Hope Step. It is the springboard from which we begin the journey toward spiritual awakening. In Step One, we felt hopeless and beaten as we surrendered. Step Two gives us new hope as we begin to see that there is help available if we simply come to believe. We no longer need to struggle alone. It is our chance to end our old patterns of behavior and emerge into a new lifestyle. Our deep desire is to become the person we were meant to be. Step Two provides us with the foundation for the spiritual growth we seek in order to achieve our fulfillment.

2. What is your interpretation of a Higher Power at this point? Describe the attributes of that Power. _____

    _____

    _____

    _____

3. The Twelve Steps have a spiritual foundation. What does this mean to you? _____

    _____

    _____

    _____

Newcomers often find two major problems with this Step. The first is a belief in a Power greater than ourselves. We may have heard or read that "faith as small as a mustard seed can work wonders." If doubt persists, we may be denying the idea of a Higher Power's healing presence. We might find it impossible to imagine that even a Higher Power could heal our obsessions and compulsions. By accepting the fact that the most devout spiritual seekers suffer from dark moments of doubt, our faith can be strengthened. Our willingness to believe and to ask to have our faith strengthened marks the beginning of our spiritual development. This is the foundation of the ACA Twelve Step Program. The second problem with this Step is the implication of insanity. Having recognized that our lives are unmanageable, we must come to terms with the fact that we need a new director. These are powerful issues and, at first, can be frightening. For many of us, they are definite contradictions of our old beliefs and lifestyle.

4. What do you hope to gain from accepting the concept of a Power greater than yourself?

    _____
    _____
    _____

5. In what areas of your life can you recognize your insane behavior? _____

    _____
    _____
    _____

6. What does "faith as small as a mustard seed can work wonders" mean to you?_____

    _____
    _____
    _____

Before entering the Program, many of us move away from the idea of anything spiritual. We don't understand it, or don't like the idea of it. Our lack of trust in others sometimes blocks our ability to accept the fact that there could be a spiritual being who could offer us support. The basis for these beliefs may lie in the fact that we have become accustomed to having our self-will dictate every action. We are self-sufficient and don't see a need for outside support. Our prayers may not have been answered, and we may have lost confidence in a Higher Power. It is possible that our self-esteem is so low that we do not feel worthy of a Higher Power. We believe that we need to do everything ourselves, and we don't trust anyone.

7. Explain how lack of trust can block your acceptance of a Higher Power._____

    _____
    _____
    _____

8. What are some experiences you remember that caused you to lose faith in God? _____

    _____
    _____
    _____

9. What are your memories of the spiritual environment in your home? How do these memories influence your beliefs today? _____

    _____

_____

_____

If we have been successful in completing Step One, we have a good foundation for accepting the concept of a Higher Power. Having surrendered our powerlessness in Step One, we have become aware that our self-will has been getting in our way. When we discover there is a Power greater than ourselves, we let go of our self-will and can find our own God.

10. How has self-will been active in your life? Describe areas in which your self-will dominates
     your actions. _____

     _____

     _____

     _____

11. What relief do you expect to feel when you become ready to let go of your self-will? _____

     _____

     _____

     _____

Many people have found that all that is required to "come to believe" is to attend meetings on a regular basis. Through the dynamics of the Program, it becomes obvious that something is working for the people at the meetings. If we are willing to keep an open mind and recognize the success that people are enjoying, the rest can happen easily.

12. What is your pattern of attending meetings? _____

     _____

     _____

     _____

13. How do you see attendance at meetings as necessary to your program? _____

     _____

     _____

     _____

Our willingness to surrender and to believe in the process helps us to replace our self-will and allows our unconscious to take over. When this happens, the idea of a Higher Power becomes acceptable to us. We shift our attention away from wanting our addictive behavior to change, and we begin to understand that life is a process. Working the Steps and being healed is a process. This shift of focus reveals the presence of a Higher Power assisting, empowering, and doing things for us that we could not possibly have managed ourselves.

14. List example of your willingness to trust in the process and surrender to the idea of
     a Higher Power being available to you. _____

     _____

_____

_____

During the beginning stages of accepting the presence of a Higher Power, it is sometimes helpful to make a game of it. We can look on chance events and coincidences in our lives as being miracles, or gifts, from our Higher Power. By taking time to thank our Higher Power for simple things, like "not getting a ticket for running a red light" or "finding a beautiful dress on sale," we can learn to accept and appreciate His presence in our lives. This may seem silly at first, but it helps us to "come to believe."

15. In what ways can you imagine yourself "playing games" in order to become familiar with the concept of a Higher Power? Site an example. _____

_____

_____

_____

Step Two does not mean that we must immediately come to believe in God as He may be presented in various religious denominations. In fact, our belief in God may come only as a result of seeing His power at work in our lives. All that is required is a willingness to believe there is a Power greater than ourselves. This Power can be whatever we choose it to be. It can be God as we understand Him, a friend, a partner, a person from the Program, or the Program itself. For some of us, God can be Love.

16. Describe your religious or spiritual beliefs. What are your reasons for believing as you do? _____

_____

_____

_____

17. Explain the God of your choice. How do you interact with this God? _____

_____

_____

_____

Belief in a Power greater than ourselves is central to becoming the happy, positive, and loving person we are truly meant to be. Inasmuch as our old ways led us into the depths of despair, we became self-centered, lonely, and detached from ourselves. We found that our reasoning mind could not solve all our problems.

18. Why is belief in a Higher Power central to our being able to lead a fully rewarding life? What relief do you expect this belief to give you? _____

_____

_____

_____

Step Two implies that we are insane. The dictionary defines insanity as "inability to manage one's own affairs and perform one's social duties" and "without recognition of one's own illness." If this is our first exposure to the Steps, we may not be totally aware of the extent of our illness. We may still be blaming outside circumstances for our condition rather than admitting responsibility for our own behavior.

19. Describe the fears in your life today. (e.g., emotional and financial insecurity, relationships, authority figures, rejection, abandonment, sex, or death) _____

_____

_____

_____

20. How do you see yourself as unable to manage your own affairs? _____

_____

_____

_____

21. What do you believe is the extent of your illness? Explain. _____

_____

_____

_____

Many of us have acquired certain characteristics and personality traits that protect us from the realities of life. Some of the more common characteristics are being defiant, self-sufficient, indifferent, resentful, self-deluded, and self-centered. These alone are an indication that we suffer from some form of insanity—that we behave insanely in many areas of our lives.

22. How do the characteristics listed above affect your ability to function normally in your current environment? _____

_____

_____

_____

In order to make changes in our lives, we must be willing to look at ourselves honestly and recognize our own degree of insanity. It is easy for the alcoholic or chemically dependent person to accept his insanity, because his addictive behavior is obviously insane. For adult children, it is more difficult to accept insanity because we are not aware of our behavior. It is easy for us to deceive ourselves and look to outside sources for the cause of our dysfunction. We have a degree of responsibility in being aware of people, places, and things that activates our insane behavior. When we break through this self-delusion, we become ready to accept our behavior as being insane in many cases.

23. List the major areas in your life that indicate you behave insanely. _____

_____

_____

_____

24. In what ways do you blame others for your behavior rather than looking at yourself?___

_____

_____

_____

As we come in contact with others and listen to their stories, we are exposed to experiences similar to ours. It becomes clear to us that we each maintain "emotional sobriety" only one day at a time and that we are in remission rather than totally cured. We must continually work at improving the quality of our lives. We eventually come to the realization that anything we do or think that is destructive to ourselves or to someone else is insane. Based on this, worry is insane, as well as depressions, compulsions, and obsessions. The mere fact that we believe we can control others is insane.

25. How do worry, depressions, obsessions, and compulsions affect your behavior?_____

_____

_____

_____

26. What are you willing to do to reduce the amount of stress in your life? _____

_____

_____

_____

27. What is your most effective tool for maintaining "emotional sobriety?"_____

_____

_____

_____

Our society as a whole is insane. We are taught from youth to do what is right, and it is expected that we know the difference between right and wrong. Based on our role models, the message as to what is right and wrong is not always clear. It is expected that we conduct ourselves responsibly and are able to manage our own lives. Since in reality we cannot manage our own lives, it must be concluded that we do not know the difference between right and wrong. When we can accept this, we are truly ready to admit that we behave insanely.

28. How did the role models in your life contribute to your condition today? _____

_____

_____

_____

_____

29. How did the role models in your life contribute to your current attitude toward life? ___

_____

_____

_____

30. What were the things most lacking in your role models? _____

_____

_____

_____

When we started this program, we may have been expecting instant results. During our childhood, it may have been common to see anger or confusion when things didn't happen "right now." In this program sudden change is the exception, not the rule. It requires patience and understanding to achieve the recovery we are looking for. Each of us is unique, and recovery begins for us at different stages in the Steps. Some of us may experience instant relief, whereas others may not begin to feel different until later in the Steps.

31. What childhood experiences have influenced your desire to have things happen "right now?" _____

_____

_____

_____

32. How have patience and understanding affected your ability to progress toward recovery?

_____

_____

_____

Coming to believe in a Higher Power and admitting our insanity require a great deal of humility. Lack of humility is what got us to the position we are in today, and it is important to practice humility in all our affairs. Humility is a recurrent theme of the Program, and our growth is enhanced by our willingness to be humble. As we attend meetings and work the Steps, we discover a peace and serenity that is possible only through our surrender and the desire to improve the quality of our lives.

33. List specific situations that show you are humble. _____

_____

_____

_____

_____

_____

_____

34. List specific situations that show you lack humility. _____
_____
_____
_____

When we become ready to accept fully our powerlessness and unmanageability (Step One), when we accept a Higher Power and our insanity (Step Two), we will be ready to take action and turn our lives over to the care of God as we understand Him (Step Three). There is no need to hurry. The important thing is that we are ready and that we have the faith necessary to proceed with the remaining Steps.

NOTES: _____
_____
_____
_____
_____
_____
_____
_____
_____
_____
_____
_____
_____
_____
_____
_____
_____
_____
_____
_____
_____

STEP THREE

MADE A DECISION TO TURN OUR WILL AND OUR LIVES OVER
TO THE CARE OF GOD AS WE UNDERSTOOD HIM

Step Three requires that we take affirmative action as a result of the developing awareness we have gained from working the first two steps. In Step One, we admitted we were powerless, that our lives had become unmanageable. In Step Two, we came to believe that a Power greater than ourselves could restore us to sanity.

1. List ways in which Step One prepared you for Step Three. _____
    _____
    _____
    _____

2. List ways in which Step Two prepared you for Step Three. _____
    _____
    _____
    _____

Step Three seems to require more of us than the first two steps because we are now asked to turn ourselves over to a Higher Power with total abandon. If we feel pressured by this decision, we are going too fast. We must slow down and take the time needed to become ready to proceed. It is in these first three steps that we set the foundation for working all of the steps and for achieving the peace and serenity we are looking for.

3. List examples that indicate you are prepared to turn your will and your life over to the care of God. _____
    _____
    _____
    _____

4. What resistance do you have that indicates you may have blocked God from your life?
    _____
    _____
    _____

The key to success in working Step Three lies in our willingness to turn our lives over to the care of God. This is difficult for many of us because we are so accustomed to handling our lives on self-will alone. Our self-will has barred God from our lives, and the idea of surrender is frightening. We learned to pray to God and to ask Him for things we want, but we were always in control. We are accustomed to asking Him for guidance in helping us achieve our goals. This is different from turning our very essence over to Him to do whatever He wants without our having any say in the matter.

5. When, where, and how does self-will appear in your life? _____

_____

_____

_____

6. What goals or objectives do you pray for that show you are asking for *your will* rather than God's will? _____

_____

_____

_____

If we have successfully worked Steps One and Two, we have accepted our situation and are ready to look for a new manager of our lives. Letting our Higher Power guide our lives becomes a little easier when we realize that we haven't done such a good job so far. Our fears and resentments become manageable when we choose God as our new director. We discover that we can impact our lives in a positive way. As we begin to rely on a Higher Power, we become willing to turn our lives over and to trust in the results.

7. What are your expectations as to the outcome of turning your life over to God's management? _____

_____

_____

_____

In the beginning stages of turning our lives over, we will possibly experience resistance. This may be attributed to our need for independence since most of us thrive on being in charge and cling to the illusion of being free to "do our own thing." We may concede only the problems that are causing us the most pain. This is usually a start, and will provide us with the confidence needed as we see that God has answers to all of our problems. As we become more comfortable with the fact that our problems do diminish, we become more willing to accept the notion of turning our entire lives over to His care.

8. Is your focus more on turning only your problems over rather than surrendering completely? Explain. _____

_____

_____

_____

9. Indicate ways in which your trust in God is deepening. _____

_____

_____

_____

Experience tells us that the more willing we are, the faster the Program will come to us, the faster we will get its meaning and be able to live it. If we try too hard consciously, we will become impatient and block our progress with frustration, irritation, resentment, and self-pity.

10. List the ways in which obsessive thinking and compulsive behavior still cause problems in your life. _____

_____

_____

_____

The central theme of Step Three is best expressed by the slogan "Let Go and Let God." The idea of letting go can help us greatly because we see that surrendering our will only allows for our further growth. We begin to realize that God takes good care of us. As long as we do the "footwork" and do not expect God to do everything for us, we will find God's will for us and be able to carry out His plan.

11. What meaning does the statement "Pray to God, but row toward shore" have for you as it relates to doing the "footwork"? _____

_____

_____

_____

Our thinking mind, using instinct and logic to bolster our ego, tells us that we will become nothing if we turn our will and our lives over to the care of God. Strange as it may seem, the more we are willing to depend on a Higher Power, the more independent we become. Our dependence on God is actually a means of gaining the true spiritual independence that we all seek.

12. Dependence on God is really a means of gaining independence. What does this mean to you?_____

_____

_____

_____

Caution is an important factor in completing this Step. If we are not completely comfortable with the idea of turning our will and our lives over to the care of God, we must slow down and do more work. Some of us may still be experiencing the powerful impact of our addictive behavior. Whatever it involves, be it relationships, money, drugs, or food, we face the prospect of spiritual as well as physical death. We began this program because the path we were on was destroying our life. This behavior was a way to temporarily numb the emotional pain, distract our boredom, or relieve us of stress. Being asked to trust in a Higher Power may present a challenge to us since we in no way can manipulate or manage God.

13. What behavior do you still feel enslaved by that prevents you from turning *all* of your life over to God? _____

_____

_____
_____

The Twelve Steps is a spiritual program. Step Three is an opportunity to let a Spiritual Power greater than us take charge of the rest of our lives. Fundamentally, this also means we may stop feeling responsible for everything and everybody. This is simply to say that the way to experience peace and serenity is to surrender.

14. Measure your present acceptance of the Twelve Steps as a spiritual program of recovery.

_____
_____
_____

It is not important to understand a Higher Power in order to let go. We need only believe in the process for our own well-being. If we are having trouble taking Step Three, it is probably because we did not successfully take Step Two. In this case, it is important to return to Step Two before proceeding.

15. What is your response to the statement "It isn't necessary (or possible) to understand God. We need only accept that the Power is there and know it can restore us to sanity?"

_____
_____
_____

16. Explain your understanding of God at this stage of your recovery. _____
_____
_____
_____

Once we are ready to take Step Three, we will see a change come over us. We will appear calmer and feel that a weight has been lifted from our shoulders. It can happen right away or gradually over a day or two as our consciousness begins to recognize that a Higher Power seems to be taking over. Don't expect to remain in this state of euphoria forever. There will be times when we take our wills back, and we need only to recognize this. There are no saints in this Program; we will have slips. However, as we continue to work the Program on a daily basis, we will see that we become more ready and willing to continually turn our lives over.

17. In what ways are you aware of your tendency to take charge of matters that would be better left to God? _____
_____
_____
_____

There is a paradox in the way this program seems to work. When we give up managing our own lives and begin to trust in God's will for us, we will find we are calmer and more accepting of things around us. Friends will compliment us on how well we are managing our lives. As we stop trying to keep ourselves on a straight and narrow path of self-discipline, people will begin to recognize how well-disciplined we are.

18. What changes have you or others noticed in your behavior that can be attributed to working the Program? _____

_____

_____

_____

Most of us who start this Program do so in search of answers to the complex questions of life and also to find a way to stop repeating painful cycles of ineffective behavior. In the past, some of us may have experimented with lifestyles and beliefs that appeared to present solutions. What we are really looking for is a personal experience of God that transcends the arguments over mankind's conflicting dogmas.

In concluding the examination of your preparedness to turn your will and life over to God, what was revealed to you about how you have:

19. **"MADE A DECISION . . ."** Have you stopped thinking about it and done it? If you haven't yet made the decision, list the things that are holding you back. _____

_____

_____

_____

20. **"TO TURN OUR WILL AND OUR LIVES OVER . . ."** Do you trust that turning over doesn't mean giving up your life? If your answer to this question is "no," explain why you feel this way. _____

_____

_____

_____

21. **"TO THE CARE OF GOD . . ."** How do you see God as caring for you?_____

_____

_____

_____

22. **"AS WE UNDERSTAND HIM . . ."** How do you understand Him now? If you are still struggling with the idea of God, what events have formed your present view? _____

_____

_____

_____

If you are prepared to take Step Three, repeat the step out loud right now. Follow your assertion of the Third Step with the AA Third Step Prayer. This prayer is a powerful way to focus your daily intention to turn your life over to the care of God.

THIRD STEP PRAYER

"God, I offer myself to Thee—to build with me and do with me as Thou wilt. Relieve me of the bondage of self, that I may better do Thy will. Take away my difficulties, that victory over them may bear witness to those I would help of Thy Power, Thy Love, and Thy Way of Life. May I do Thy Will always."[1]

THIRD STEP GIFT

Striving for recognition . . .
An apprearance of superiority . . .
Accomplishment . . .
A relationship that fits my pictures.
All a mirage, relentless . . .
Thirsting to fill the emptiness within . . .
Incessantly demanding more
and more.
Yet—ever present, within,
serene and uncritical . . .
Poised in the gentle stillness
of infinite patience . . .
Spirit . . .
My Higher Power . . .
Comforting love . . .
Awaits.

1. Alcoholics Anonymous, Alcoholics Anonymous World Services, Inc., (New York), p.63.

NOTES:

HIGHER POWER EXERCISE

The purpose of this writing exercise is to deepen your contact with your own Higher Power (Inner Wisdom, Higher Self). This process works best when you can write uninterrupted for a period of time and when you can be quiet and meditative with soft music playing.

Don't look for anything profound as a result of doing this exercise. This is an opportunity to discover a special part of you and say "hello." The growth of your relationship with your Higher Power will take place as you acknowledge its existence and call on your Higher Power for guidance.

There are six stages involved in completing this process. Each builds on the other, so follow the sequence as listed for best results.

LIFE SEGMENTS

Use the Higher Power worksheet (LIFE SEGMENTS) to divide your life into ten-year segments. In each segment, list the heroes you worshipped, wisdom figures you thought to be wise, or people you admired and wanted to imitate. They can be people you have known personally, either living or dead. They can be people you have never known—mythical, historical, or religious figures, characters from books, TV, or movies.

> EXAMPLES: Parent, grandparent, aunt; Jesus Christ, Virgin Mary, saint, priest, rabbi; Buddha, Greek Gods, prophet; teacher, coach, political figure; Billy Graham, Joan of Arc, John F. Kennedy, Martin Luther King; animals, objects.

Note briefly the specialness about each figure and what you received from them.

SPECIALNESS RECEIVED

Transfer the list of special things you received from these figures to the Higher Power worksheet (SPECIALNESS RECEIVED).

MEDITATION

After completing the above, sit quietly, meditate, and listen to the music. Use the image of a kaleidoscope. Close your eyes and let all of the figures you have cherished blend together. Don't try to think up an image; just let it happen. Trust that it will come to you without any effort on your part. Accept that the image is forming in your mind at this moment. Now relax and see within yourself your own Higher Power. Let your creative mind present you with an image of all those special people that you have known or related to. Let your imagination create that special someone or something that makes you feel quiet, safe, accepted, understood, loved, and supported—that someone or something with whom you can share everything about yourself without reservation.

RESULTS OF MEDITATION

Begin slowly to open your eyes and return to the present. When you are ready, without interruption, draw a picture or describe in writing the Higher Power that you discovered as a result of this experience. List the qualities that your Higher Power has that are meaningful to you.

DIALOGUE WITH YOUR HIGHER POWER

There is a final step necessary to get in touch with your Higher Power. Since your Higher Power is not part of your intellect, He cannot be contacted by thinking. Relax for a moment and pretend your mind is a tape recorder. Run a cleaning tape through it so that all thoughts and concerns are erased from your mind. There is no need to think about anything. Relax and let your mind go blank. Wait for whatever comes to mind and write it down without worrying about it.

Let your hand do the writing. Record what you hear or feel spontaneously. Nothing is irrelevant; try to capture every word and image that occurs to you. It may seem silly, nonsensical, or embarrassing, but write it anyway. Write fast so that you don't have time to think about what you are doing. Don't take time to censor or to make sense of your writing.

Some suggestions that may help you in this process are as follows:

1. Avoid looking at the page.
2. Close your eyes while writing.
3. Ignore punctuation rules.
4. Write with your other hand as a means of keeping out of your head.
5. Allow dialogue to develop. You are the pen through which your Higher Power is communicating and responding to questions.

Limit writing to approximately 15 minutes.

HIGHER POWER WORKSHEET

LIFE SEGMENTS

EXAMPLE	1-10	11-20	21-30
GRANDFATHER Love Playtime Walks Advice			
31-40	**41-50**	**51-60**	**61-70**

SPECIALNESS RECEIVED DURING LIFE SEGMENTS

Love _____   _____

Advice _____   _____

Playfulness _____   _____

_____   _____

_____   _____

_____   _____

_____   _____

_____   _____

_____   _____

_____   _____

_____   _____

_____   _____

_____   _____

_____   _____

_____   _____

_____   _____

_____   _____

_____   _____

_____   _____

_____   _____

_____   _____

STEP FOUR

MADE A SEARCHING AND FEARLESS MORAL INVENTORY OF OURSELVES

Our introduction to the ACA Program occurs as a result of a series of very painful events brought about by the external pressures of reality. The pain of this reality has weakened the defenses that comprise our denial system, and we are forced to look at ourselves and see the consequences of our addictive behavior. Our shock and our acknowledgment of the serious problems in our lives form the beginning of an adventure in self-discovery and recovery. We start facing ourselves and uncovering our acquired character defects. When we accept the fact that these character defects are acquired, we can come to terms with how they have controlled us in the past, and then we can let go of them.

1. What anxieties do you have about preparing your inventory? _____
   _____
   _____
   _____

As part of this process, we become aware of the denial that has protected us from the reality of our addictive behavior and preserved our limited sense of self-worth and dignity. Step Four will help us to deal with our denial system, which has been one of our major survival techniques. Denial has distorted our perception and impaired our judgment so that we have become self-deluded and incapable of accurate self-awareness.

2. How do you see denial as being one of your survival techniques? _____
   _____
   _____
   _____

3. Describe your behavior when you are in denial. _____
   _____
   _____
   _____

Denial is the core component of our illness. To a greater or lesser extent, it can be found in all of us. It can be the fatal aspect of our illness because it keeps us locked into an increasingly destructive pattern. It consists of many defenses and maneuvers that we use to protect ourselves from the reality of our condition. Step Four is a helpful tool for penetrating our denial system, and it provides us with an opportunity to learn a great deal about our illness and its consequences. Denial is seen in many different forms and operates in various ways, some of which are as follows:
   A. Pretending that something does not exist when in reality it does.
   B. Being willing to admit there is a problem but unwilling to see the severity of it.
   C. Seeing the problem as being caused by something or someone else. The behavior is not denied, but its cause is someone else's responsibility.
   D. Offering excuses, alibis, justifications, and other explanations for behavior.
   E. Dealing with the problem on a general level, avoiding personal and emotional

awareness of the situation or conditions.

    F.   Changing the subject to avoid threatening topics.

    G.   Becoming angry and irritable when reference is made to the condition. This helps to avoid the issue.

4. In what environments is denial most active? (e.g., family, work, social relationships) ____

_____

_____

_____

During the first three steps, we faced many changes in our lives. In Step One, we admitted that we were powerless, that our lives had become unmanageable. In Step Two, we came to believe in a Higher Power as a means of restoring our sanity. In Step Three, we made a decision to turn our will and our lives over to the care of God as we understood Him.

5. Review Step One and list any areas in which you are having difficulty accepting the idea of powerlessness and unmanageability. _____

_____

_____

_____

6. Review Step Two and list any areas in which you are having difficulty accepting the idea of a Higher Power and your insanity. _____

_____

_____

_____

7. Review Step Three and list any areas in which you are having difficulty accepting the idea of turning your will and your life over to the care of God. _____

_____

_____

_____

An inventory is not a history. It relates to what is on hand at the moment. It is a list of things in stock now and does not concern what was there in the past. Looking at the inventory this way, it is easier to make it a fearless inventory because we have no reason to fear the present. Writing is important and is a key to success in working Step Four. As we list our qualities, we will discover both good and bad traits that will amaze us. It is important not to judge ourselves but rather to recognize that our main goal is to accept what we discover.

8. What is your interpretation of a fearless inventory? _____

_____

_____

_____

As we more completely understand the childhood origin of much of our behavior, we will develop a mature perspective on our being adult children. Understanding our behavior is only part of the task we are faced with in reaching our inner child. We have no doubt identified some of our childhood behaviors, and we understand them to be dysfunctional. However, we continue to repeat them unconsciously and are frustrated by their reappearance. This can be likened to gardeners continually lopping off tops of weeds that, just as persistently, regrow from the roots. They didn't seem to comprehend the whole job, which was to get to the roots that lay hidden beneath the surface. Step Four uncovers many childhood roots that can be dealt with through the help of our Higher Power. This process is a vital key to our personal transformation.

9. Which of your childhood behaviors do you most often repeat? _____

   _____

   _____

   _____

10. How is understanding your behavior helping you get to know your inner child?_____

   _____

   _____

   _____

Two of the linkpins that hold our problem behavior in place are resentment and fear. They have had a strong impact on our childhood, and we still find them deeply influencing our adult behavior. Resentment, among other feelings of unexpressed anger, is thought to be the source from which many mental and physical ills originate. Going through life with deep resentments can only result in futility and unhappiness. If we allow our resentments (fancied or real) to dominate us, they have the power to destroy us.

11. List three major resentments you have toward people, institutions, or principles. _____

   _____

   _____

   _____

The destructive power of fear is equally detrimental and corrosive to the fabric of our lives. At this point in our recovery, we may find fear in all our behaviors. Whatever its origin, given a particular situation in our daily lives (e.g., fear of abandonment or authority figures), fear will set in motion a sequence of circumstances that will bring about a misfortune we feel we don't deserve. As we inventory our fears, we may find that their presence is particularly evident when our self-reliance fails us. Our belief may be that if we only had enough self-confidence, we wouldn't have this problem. Here, again, our self-delusion is dangerous. If we have sincerely taken Step Three, we are now prepared to trust and rely upon an infinite God instead of our finite selves.

12. List three major fears you have toward people, institutions, or principles. _____

   _____

   _____

   _____

Being willing to face our resentments and fears takes courage. However, our faith in our Higher Power is the tap root through which we will let Him demonstrate what He can do. The spiritual sickness that is tied to resentment and fear is the malady we can overcome by sincerely working these Steps with our Higher Power. Having a spiritual healing will straighten out the crippling mental and physical conditions of our lives.

13. How can your relationship with your Higher Power help you to overcome your resentments and fears? _____

_____

_____

_____

Step Four provides a means for viewing ourselves honestly, possibly for the first time. This can be the beginning of a new awareness of ourselves. Some of the discoveries may be overwhelming to us. In that case, we need only turn the responsibility for acceptance of ourselves over to our Higher Power. If we have successfully worked Steps One through Three, this should be relatively easy.

14. What difficulties might you encounter in attempting to look at yourself honestly and recognize who you really are? _____

_____

_____

_____

As we prepare our Fourth Step inventory, we will be looking at our character traits and seeing our strengths and weaknesses. Our strengths are seen in behavior that has positive effects on ourselves as well as on others. Our weaknesses manifest themselves in behavior that is destructive to ourselves and to others. Before we can correct our problem areas, we need to examine and acknowledge our weaknesses. This understanding lies in discovering how we talk to ourselves—the ideas, beliefs, and attitudes that govern how we act.

15. What do you consider to be your main strengths? _____

_____

_____

_____

16. What do you consider to be your main weaknesses? _____

_____

_____

_____

The inventory you will be preparing is for your own benefit. It can be a tool for making a major breakthrough in your recovery and for setting you on the road to freedom. As you write the inventory, certain feelings may arise. If you notice that you are having difficulty being completely honest, denial may still be at work. Stop for a moment and reflect on what your true feelings are. Take time to "tune in" to your true feelings so that you can rid yourself of the excess baggage you have been carrying for an indefinite period of time. Remember that your Higher Power is with you and is prepared to offer the support and guidance you need to complete this work.

17. What are your current feelings toward preparing your inventory? (e.g., fear, anger, judgment)_____

_____

_____

_____

IMPORTANT GUIDELINES IN PREPARING YOUR INVENTORY

The material offered in this Fourth Step Inventory Guide is somewhat different from the inventory guides used in other Twelve Step Programs. The emphasis is on the character defects most commonly seen in adult children. When preparing the inventory, choose behavior traits that specifically apply to you. Use recent events and record words and actions as accurately as possible.

The inventory begins with an exercise on resentment and fear, followed by a series of character traits to be examined. This process enables you to prepare you for your Fifth Step. You are the primary beneficiary of your honesty and thoroughness in this inventory.

It is important not to write in generalities. As you will note in the example provided for "Isolation", being specific is helpful in identifying where the trait is active. When you list specific examples of your behavior, include WHO, WHEN, WHERE, WHAT. As part of being specific, give the names of all persons involved in the situation with you (WHO). Record the date this behavior took place (WHEN). Indicate where this behavior took place (WHERE). Finally, describe your behavior and tell what you did (WHAT).

Remember, the work you are doing as part of this Step is a demonstration of your faith that your Higher Power can do for you what you cannot do for yourself.

RESENTMENT EXERCISE

Resentment is a source of all forms of spiritual disease. Our mental and physical ills are the result of this unwholesome condition. Learning to deal with resentment is an important part of our recovery process.

List situations in which resentment is a problem for you. Answer the following questions when describing these conditions.

  a. What or who do you resent? (e.g., people, institutions, principles)
  b. Why are you resentful? (e.g., What happened to cause this resentment?)
  c. How has this resentment affected you? (e.g., self-esteem, finances, goals, relationships, sex, physical harm or threats)
  d. What character defect is active? (e.g., approval seeking, control, abandonment)

EXAMPLE: (a) I RESENT my boss (b) BECAUSE he doesn't care to hear my story about why I am depressed. (c) THIS AFFECTS my self-esteem. (d) THIS ACTIVATES unexpressed anger and approval seeking.

1. (a) _____
    (b) _____
    (c) _____
    (d) _____
2. (a) _____
    (b) _____
    (c) _____
    (d) _____
3. (a) _____
    (b) _____
    (c) _____
    (d) _____
4. (a) _____
    (b) _____
    (c) _____
    (d) _____
5. (a) _____
    (b) _____
    (c) _____
    (d) _____
6. (a) _____
    (b) _____
    (c) _____
    (d) _____

FEAR EXERCISE

Fear is a source of all forms of spiritual disease. Our mental and physical ills are the result of this unwholesome condition. Learning to deal with fear is an important part of our recovery process.

List situations in which fear is a problem for you. Answer the following questions when describing these conditions.
   a. What or who do you fear? (e.g., people, institutions, principles)
   b. Why are you fearful? (e.g., What happened to cause this fear?)
   c. How has this fear affected you? (e.g., self-esteem, finances, goals, relationships, sex, physical harm or threats)
   d. What character defect is active? (e.g., approval seeking, control, abandonment)

EXAMPLE: (a) I FEAR my spouse (b) BECAUSE I can never please him. (c) THIS AFFECTS my self-esteem and sexuality. (d) THIS ACTIVATES my fear of abandonment.

1. (a)_____
    (b)_____
    (c)_____
    (d)_____
2. (a)_____
    (b)_____
    (c)_____
    (d)_____
3. (a)_____
    (b)_____
    (c)_____
    (d)_____
4. (a)_____
    (b)_____
    (c)_____
    (d)_____
5. (a)_____
    (b)_____
    (c)_____
    (d)_____
6. (a)_____
    (b)_____
    (c)_____
    (d)_____

CHARACTER TRAITS (WEAKNESSES)

Below is an example to assist you in completing the questions asked about the traits. Be as thorough as possible. Use additional pages as needed.

ISOLATION

1. List specific examples of your behavior that indicate you are isolating yourself.
   a. I turned down an invitation to Sharon's party last Saturday, because I feared being able to participate.
   b. I felt bashful at work when George, my supervisor, asked me why I did not actively participate in the Monday morning management meeting.

2. What do you believe is the underlying cause of this behavior? (e.g., fear, resentment, anger, guilt)
   a. I am afraid to be less than perfect and let myself go. This inhibits my ability to have fun. I worry about not fitting in as well as being noticed.
   b. I fear personal criticism if I express myself freely. Instead, I isolate myself by not speaking up.

3. What is being hurt, threatened, or interfered with? (e.g., self-esteem, goals, security, personal or sexual relations)
   a. My self-esteem is affected when I expose myself to others. I judge myself without mercy. This interferes with my desire to have a love relationship and meet new people.
   b. I feel my job security is at risk.

CHARACTER TRAITS (STRENGTHS)

Below is an example to assist you in completing the questions asked about the traits. Be as thorough as possible. Use additional pages as needed.

RECOVERY FROM ISOLATION

1. List specific examples of your behavior that indicate you isolate yourself less frequently.

    a. Today I went to lunch with Diane and Evelyn. I felt comfortable and at ease and was able to share in the conversation. I took a risk and shared some special feelings about my desire to be in an intimate relationship. I did not feel threatened by sharing this.

    b. During last Monday's management meeting I expressed a concern relative to rising business expenses. Rather than be criticized, I was acknowledged for taking the time to provide the information.

2. What do you hope to achieve as you become more confident about situations in which you would usually isolate yourself?

    a. I want to cultivate new, healthy relationships which will help me to feel more comfortable in social settings. I hope to become more flexible so that I can learn to be spontaneous and have fun.

    b. I want to become more assertive and expressive in business settings. I believe this will be an opportunity to actualize my full potential.

ANGER

DESCRIPTION

Anger is a major source of many of our problems. It is a feeling that we often suppress because it is so uncomfortable for us. In our chaotic homes, the turmoil was so intense that we learned to deny our anger. We felt safer not expressing our anger and hoped it would go away. We eventually became unaware of its presence. Repressed anger leads to serious resentment and depression. It causes physical complications that lead to stress-related illnesses. Denying anger causes problems in relationships because we are not being truthful about our feelings. We are fearful of alienating people and destroying relationships.

FEELINGS AND BEHAVIOR

1. RESENTMENT
2. SELF-PITY
3. JEALOUSY
4. PREJUDICE

5. DEPRESSION
6. SADNESS
7. PHYSICAL ILLNESS

1. List specific examples of your behavior that indicate you are angry. _____

_____

_____

_____

_____

_____

2. What do you believe is the underlying cause of this behavior? (e.g., resentment, anxiety, guilt, insecurity) _____

_____

_____

_____

_____

_____

3. What is being hurt, threatened, or interfered with? (e.g., self-esteem, goals, security, personal or sexual relations)_____

_____

_____

_____

_____

_____

RECOVERY FROM ANGER

DESCRIPTION

Learning to express anger is a major step toward recovery. It releases us from a lot of hidden emotions and allows healing to take place. Expressing anger is a vehicle for setting boundaries and helps us to be honest with ourselves. As we become willing to express anger honestly, we find that we move beyond the emotion and that we are better able to cope with the situation. Our relationships improve as we begin to feel safe in expressing ourselves. Stress-related problems diminish, and we feel better physically.

FEELINGS AND BEHAVIOR

1. EXPRESS ANGER
2. IDENTIFY TRUE FEELINGS
3. MAKE REASONABLE REQUESTS

4. SET BOUNDARIES
5. INNER CALM AND PEACE

1. List specific examples of your behavior that indicate you are expressing anger in a healthy way. _____

    _____

    _____

    _____

    _____

    _____

    _____

    _____

    _____

    _____

2. What do you hope to achieve as you identify and release your anger? _____

    _____

    _____

    _____

    _____

    _____

    _____

    _____

    _____

    _____

    _____

    _____

APPROVAL SEEKING

DESCRIPTION

As a result of our dysfunctional upbringing, we fear disapproval and criticism. What we wanted so desperately as children was to receive approval from our parents, grandparents, siblings, and significant others. This occurred rarely for most of us, so we were constantly seeking validation of ourselves. The need for validation continues into adulthood and manifests itself in the way we pattern our behavior around the desires of others. This behavior keeps us out of touch with our true feelings and causes us to be insecure. It prevents us from discovering our own wants and needs. We are always on the lookout for others' reactions and attempt to manage their impressions of us. We constantly please everyone and remain loyal to extremes.

FEELINGS AND BEHAVIOR

1. ABANDONMENT OF SELF
2. DISHONESTY
3. IMPRESSION MANAGEMENT
4. FEAR OF FAILURE
5. EXTREME LOYALTY
6. PEOPLE PLEASING
7. FEAR OF PERSONAL CRITICISM
8. IGNORING OUR OWN NEEDS
9. INSECURITY (LACK OF CONFIDENCE)

1. List specific examples of your behavior that indicate you are seeking approval. _____
   _____
   _____
   _____
   _____
   _____

2. What do you believe is the underlying cause of this behavior? (e.g., fear, insecurity) _____
   _____
   _____
   _____
   _____
   _____

3. What areas are being hurt, threatened, or interfered with? (e.g., self-esteem, goals, security, personal or sexual relations)_____
   _____
   _____
   _____
   _____

RECOVERY FROM APPROVAL SEEKING

DESCRIPTION

We begin to rely on our own approval and on that of our Higher Power. We understand that wanting approval is okay, but we no longer need to seek approval, or validation, from outside sources. We accept compliments from others and learn to simply say thank you, believing that the compliment is sincere. We say yes when it feels comfortable, and we are willing to say no when it doesn't feel right.

FEELINGS AND BEHAVIOR

1. RECOGNIZE OUR OWN NEEDS
2. TELL THE TRUTH ABOUT HOW WE FEEL
3. SELF-LOYALTY
4. SECURITY IN BEING OURSELVES

1. List specific examples of your behavior that indicate you are not seeking approval. ____

_____

_____

_____

_____

_____

_____

_____

_____

_____

_____

2. What do you hope to achieve as your need for approval lessens? ____

_____

_____

_____

_____

_____

_____

_____

_____

_____

_____

_____

_____

CARETAKING

DESCRIPTION

As long as we take care of others, solve their problems, and supply their needs, we are not required to look at ourselves. As this trait becomes more pronounced, we lose our own identity. As children, we took on the concerns and problems of others far beyond our years and, in many cases, were deprived of a normal childhood. The attention we got caused us to believe we had God-like powers. Taking care of others boosted our self-esteem and made us feel indispensable. It gave purpose to our life. As caretakers, we are most comfortable with chaotic situations in which we can be reassured that we are needed. We often end up as martyrs and never experience the joy of taking care of ourselves.

FEELINGS AND BEHAVIOR

1. HELP AND SEEK "VICTIMS"
2. RESCUE PEOPLE
3. IGNORE OUR NEEDS
4. SUPER-RESPONSIBLE
5. MAKE OURSELVES INDISPENSABLE
6. MARTYRDOM
7. LOSS OF IDENTITY

1. List specific examples of your behavior that indicate you are being a caretaker. _____

_____

_____

_____

_____

_____

2. What do you believe is the underlying cause of this behavior? (e.g., guilt, low self-esteem, resentment, anxiety) _____

_____

_____

_____

_____

_____

3. What is being hurt, threatened, or interfered with? (e.g., self-esteem, goals, security, personal or sexual relations) _____

_____

_____

_____

_____

_____

RECOVERY FROM CARETAKING

DESCRIPTION

As we leave the role of caretaker, we stop being responsible for everyone and allow each individual to find his own way. We understand that everyone has a Higher Power, which is the best source for guidance, love, and support. We become free from the burden of meeting everyone's needs and find time to develop our own personalities. Our obsession to care for others is replaced with the acceptance that we are powerless over the lives of others and that our only responsibility in life is for our own welfare and happiness.

FEELINGS AND BEHAVIOR

1. STOP RESCUING
2. LEARN TO CARE FOR OURSELVES
3. SET BOUNDARIES
4. DEVELOP OWN IDENTITY
5. DETACH FROM "VICTIM" RELATIONSHIPS

1. List specific examples of your behavior that indicate you are not being a caretaker. ____

_____
_____
_____
_____
_____
_____
_____
_____

2. What do you hope to achieve as you become more aware of your needs and stop being a caretaker?_____

_____
_____
_____
_____
_____
_____
_____
_____
_____

CONTROL

DESCRIPTION

As children, we had little control over our environment or the events that took place in our lives. As adults, we control our feelings and behavior, and we try to control the feelings and behavior of others. We become rigid, manipulative, and we lack spontaneity in our lives. There is an element of distrust in our need to control. We trust only ourselves to carry out a task or to handle a situation. We manipulate others in order to manage their impressions of us, and we keep a balance that feels safe for us. We fear that our lives will get worse if we let go of control. We become stressed and anxious when control is not possible.

FEELINGS AND BEHAVIOR

1. OVERREACTION TO CHANGE
2. RIGIDITY
3. INTOLERANCE
4. FEAR OF FAILURE
5. JUDGMENTALISM
6. LACK OF TRUST
7. DIFFICULTY HAVING FUN
8. MANIPULATION OF OTHERS

1. List specific examples of your behavior that indicate you are attempting to control or manipulate people or situations. _____

_____

_____

_____

_____

_____

2. What do you believe is the underlying cause of this behavior? (e.g., fear, insecurity, lack of trust, resentment, anger)_____

_____

_____

_____

_____

_____

3. What is being hurt, threatened, or interfered with? (e.g., self-esteem, goals, security, personal or sexual relations)_____

_____

_____

_____

_____

_____

RECOVERY FROM CONTROL

DESCRIPTION

As we become more aware of our controlling behavior, we realize that we are powerless and that we have no control over anything or anyone except ourselves. We stop manipulating situations in an effort to get our way, and we begin accepting our Higher Power as the ultimate source of security. As we begin to surrender our will and our lives to the care of God, we eliminate a great deal of stress and anxiety. We become willing to participate without being concerned about the outcome. Recital of the Serenity Prayer can be a helpful tool in correcting our desire to control.

FEELINGS AND BEHAVIOR

1. ACCEPTANCE OF CHANGE
2. TRUST IN PEOPLE
3. LET GO
4. REDUCTION IN STRESS LEVELS
5. LEARN TO HAVE FUN
6. ACCEPT OTHERS AS THEY ARE

1. List specific examples of your behavior that indicate you no longer feel a need to be in control. _____

_____
_____
_____
_____
_____
_____
_____
_____

2. What do you hope to achieve as you become less controlling? _____

_____
_____
_____
_____
_____
_____
_____
_____
_____

FEAR OF ABANDONMENT

DESCRIPTION

As children, we observed unpredictable behavior. Never knowing from one day to the next whether our parents would be there, many of us were abandoned either physically or emotionally. Fear of abandonment was a pattern established in early childhood because of our desperate attempts to please our parents. However, as their addiction increased in severity, we simply did not exist. As adults, we choose partners with whom we can re-enact this fear. By trying hard to be perfect and to meet our partner's needs, we avoid conflicts in order to avoid experiencing the pain of our past. Reducing this pain takes precedence over dealing with the issues, or conflicts, and creates an environment of tension and poor communication.

FEELINGS AND BEHAVIOR

1. INSECURITY
2. CARETAKING
3. CO-DEPENDENCY

4. WORRY
5. FEELING GUILTY WHEN STANDING UP FOR OURSELVES

1. List specific examples of your behavior that indicate you fear abandonment. _____

_____

_____

_____

_____

_____

_____

2. What do you believe is the underlying cause of this behavior? (e.g., inadequacy, jealousy, need to be needed)_____

_____

_____

_____

_____

_____

_____

3. What areas are being hurt, threatened, or interfered with? (e.g., self-esteem, goals, security, personal or sexual relations)_____

_____

_____

_____

_____

_____

RECOVERY FROM FEAR OF ABANDONMENT

DESCRIPTION

By relying upon the ever-present love of our Higher Power, our self-worth increases; our fear of, and need for, abandonment diminishes. We seek out healthy relationships with people who love and take care of themselves. We feel more secure in revealing our feelings. We transfer our old dependence on others to our Higher Power. We learn to understand and accept a nurturing and loving fellowship in ACA. Our self-confidence grows as we begin to realize that we will never again be totally alone.

FEELINGS AND BEHAVIOR

1. TRUE EXPRESSIONS OF
    FEELINGS
2. SELF-CONFIDENCE

3. CONSIDER OUR OWN NEEDS
    IN A RELATIONSHIP
4. REDUCE OUR CARETAKING
    AND CO-DEPENDENCY TRAITS

1. List specific examples of your behavior that indicate you no longer fear abandonment.

    _____

    _____

    _____

    _____

    _____

    _____

    _____

    _____

    _____

2. What goals do you hope to achieve as your fears of abandonment lessen? _____

    _____

    _____

    _____

    _____

    _____

    _____

    _____

    _____

    _____

FEAR OF PEOPLE AND AUTHORITY FIGURES

DESCRIPTION

Unwarranted fear of people in roles of authority is a result of low self-esteem. We are unable to deal with people whom we perceive as being in a position of power. Common assertiveness displayed by people is often misinterpreted by us as anger. This can cause us to feel intimidated and to become oversensitive. No matter how competent we are, we compare ourselves to others and often conclude that we are inadequate. As a result, we accept compromise and avoid confrontation or criticism.

FEELINGS AND BEHAVIOR

1. FEAR OF REJECTION
2. OVERSENSITIVITY
3. SELF-ESTEEM (PRIDE)

4. COMPARING
5. REACT RATHER THAN ACT
6. INADEQUACY

1. List specific examples of your behavior that indicate you fear people and authority figures. _____

_____

_____

_____

_____

_____

2. What do you believe is the underlying cause of this behavior? (e.g., resentment, anxiety, anger, guilt, insecurity) _____

_____

_____

_____

_____

_____

3. What is being hurt, threatened, or interfered with? (e.g., self-esteem, goals, security, personal or sexual relations)_____

_____

_____

_____

_____

_____

RECOVERY FROM FEAR OF PEOPLE AND AUTHORITY FIGURES

DESCRIPTION

As we begin to feel comfortable and involved with people and authority figures, we stop focusing on pleasing and begin to behave as our true selves. We then recognize everyone as being like us, with their own fears, defenses, and insecurities. Others' behavior (assertiveness, etc.) no longer dictates how we feel about ourselves. We start acting rather than reacting when responding to others. We recognize that our ultimate authority figure is our Higher Power, who is always with us.

FEELINGS AND BEHAVIOR

1. INCREASED SELF-ESTEEM
2. STAND UP FOR OURSELVES
3. ACCEPT CONSTRUCTIVE CRITICISM
4. INTERACT WITH PEOPLE AND AUTHORITY FIGURES

1. List specific examples of your behavior that indicate you are gaining confidence around people and authority figures. _____

_____

_____

_____

_____

_____

_____

_____

2. What do you hope to achieve as you become confident and secure around people and authority figures? _____

_____

_____

_____

_____

_____

_____

_____

FROZEN FEELINGS

DESCRIPTION

Many of us have difficulty expressing feelings or even realizing that we have feelings. We harbor deep emotional pain and a deeply felt sense of guilt. As children, our feelings were met with disapproval, anger, and rejection. As a means of survival, we learned to hide our feelings or repress them entirely. As adults, we are not in touch with our feelings. We can only experience "acceptable" feelings in order to be safe. Feelings are distorted so that we can protect ourselves from reality. Distorted and repressed feelings cause resentment, anger, and depression, which eventually lead to physical illness.

FEELINGS AND BEHAVIOR

1. OUT OF TOUCH WITH FEELINGS
2. DISTORTED FEELINGS
3. SUPPRESSED FEELINGS
4. AVOIDANCE OF FEELINGS
5. PHYSICAL ILLNESS

1. List specific examples of your behavior that indicate you are not expressing your feelings.

   _____

   _____

   _____

   _____

   _____

2. What do you believe is the underlying cause of this behavior? (e.g., fear, resentment, guilt, anger, depression) _____

   _____

   _____

   _____

   _____

   _____

3. What is being hurt, threatened, or interfered with? (e.g., self-esteem, goals, security, personal or sexual relations)_____

   _____

   _____

   _____

   _____

   _____

   _____

RECOVERY FROM FROZEN FEELINGS

DESCRIPTION

As we get in touch with our feelings and learn to express them, wonderful things begin to happen. Our stress levels decrease, and we begin to see ourselves as worthwhile people. We learn that expression of feelings is a great way to communicate, and we find that our needs can be met. All we have to do is ask. As we begin to release our feelings, we experience some levels of pain. But the pain goes away, and we develop a sense of peace and serenity. The more willing we are to take risks in releasing our emotions, the more effective our recovery will be.

FEELINGS AND BEHAVIOR

1. FACING REALITY
2. OPEN EXPRESSION OF FEELINGS
3. ABILITY TO CRY
4. EXPRESS NEEDS TO OTHERS

1. List specific examples of your behavior that indicate you are learning to be aware of your feelings and to express them. _____

_____

_____

_____

_____

_____

_____

_____

_____

2. What do you hope to achieve as you become more comfortable expressing your feelings?

_____

_____

_____

_____

_____

_____

_____

_____

_____

_____

ISOLATION

DESCRIPTION

We find it safe in many instances to detach ourselves from surroundings that are uncomfortable to us. By isolating ourselves, we are preventing others from seeing us as we really are. We tell ourselves that we are not worthy and, therefore, do not deserve anything. We also tell ourselves that we cannot be punished or hurt if we don't express our feelings. Rather than take risks, we choose to procrastinate, thereby eliminating the need to face an uncertain outcome.

FEELINGS AND BEHAVIOR

1. FEAR OF REJECTION
2. FEEL DIFFERENT FROM OTHERS
3. NON-ASSERTIVENESS

4. DEFEATISM
5. LONELINESS
6. PROCRASTINATION

1. List specific examples of your behavior that indicate you are isolating yourself. _____

_____

_____

_____

_____

_____

_____

2. What do you believe is the underlying cause of this behavior? (e.g., fear, resentment, anger, guilt) _____

_____

_____

_____

_____

_____

_____

3. What is being hurt, threatened, or interfered with? (e.g., self-esteem, goals, security, personal or sexual relations)_____

_____

_____

_____

_____

_____

_____

RECOVERY FROM ISOLATION

DESCRIPTION

As we begin to feel better about ourselves, we become willing to take risks and to expose ourselves to new surroundings. We seek out friends and relationships that are nurturing, safe, and supportive. We learn to participate and to have fun in group activities. It becomes easier to express our feelings as we develop a higher sense of self-esteem. We recognize that people will accept us for who we really are. Our self-acceptance allows us to experience the precious gift of life.

FEELINGS AND BEHAVIOR

1. SELF-ACCEPTANCE
2. FREE EXPRESSION OF EMOTION
3. CULTIVATE MUTUALLY SUPPORTIVE RELATIONSHIPS
4. COMPLETE PROJECTS
5. ACTIVE PARTICIPATION IN FUNCTIONS

1. List specific examples of your behavior that indicate you isolate yourself less frequently.

_____
_____
_____
_____
_____
_____
_____
_____
_____

2. What do you hope to achieve as you feel more confident about situations from which you would usually isolate yourself?_____

_____
_____
_____
_____
_____
_____
_____
_____
_____

LOW SELF-ESTEEM

DESCRIPTION

Low self-esteem is rooted in our early childhood, during which we never felt quite adequate. As a result of constant criticism, we believed that we were bad and that we were the cause of many of the family problems. In order to feel accepted, we tried harder to please. The harder we tried, the more frustrated we became. Low self-esteem affects our ability to set and achieve goals, and so we are afraid to take risks. We feel responsible for things that go wrong, and when something goes right, we do not give ourselves credit. Instead, we feel undeserving and believe it is not going to last.

FEELINGS AND BEHAVIOR

1. NON-ASSERTIVENESS
2. FEAR OF FAILURE
3. INADEQUACY
4. FEAR OF REJECTION

5. ISOLATION
6. NEGATIVE SELF-IMAGE
7. PERFECTIONISM

1. List specific examples of your behavior that indicate you have low self-esteem. _____
   _____
   _____
   _____
   _____
   _____

2. What do you believe is the underlying cause of this behavior? (e.g., fear, resentment, anger, guilt) _____
   _____
   _____
   _____
   _____
   _____

3. What is being hurt, threatened, or interfered with? (e.g., goals, security, personal or sexual relations) _____
   _____
   _____
   _____
   _____
   _____

RECOVERY FROM LOW SELF-ESTEEM

DESCRIPTION

As we build confidence in our abilities, our self-esteem increases. We are able to interact with others and to accept ourselves for who we really are. We see our good qualities, as well as our bad, and we learn to love ourselves. We become willing to take risks, and we realize we can achieve many things that we had never dreamed possible. Sharing feelings with others becomes more comfortable, and we feel safe allowing people to know us. Relationships become healthier because we no longer look to others for validation.

FEELINGS AND BEHAVIOR

1. SELF-CONFIDENCE
2. ASSERTIVENESS
3. INTERACT WITH OTHERS

4. SELF-LOVE
5. EXPRESS FEELINGS
6. TAKE RISKS

1. List specific examples of your behavior that indicate your self-esteem is improving. ____

_____

2. What do you hope to achieve as you feel better about yourself? ____

_____

OVERDEVELOPED SENSE OF RESPONSIBILITY

DESCRIPTION

As children in a dysfunctional home, we felt responsible for what happened. We tried to be "model children" in order to solve our parents' problems. We developed the belief that we are responsible for the emotions and actions of others; even the outcome of events. We are hypersensitive to the needs of others, and we make an effort to take responsibility for others. It is important to us to be as perfect as possible. We volunteer to do things so that people will appreciate us. Our sense of responsibility causes us to overcommit, and we have a tendency to assume more than we are capable of handling.

FEELINGS AND BEHAVIOR

1. TAKE LIFE TOO SERIOUSLY
2. RIGIDITY
3. FALSE PRIDE
4. IRRESPONSIBLE
5. HIGH ACHIEVER
6. SUPER-RESPONSIBLE
7. PERFECTIONISM

1. List specific examples of your behavior that indicate you are being overresponsible. _____

_____

_____

_____

_____

_____

2. What do you believe is the underlying cause of this behavior? (e.g., fear, perfectionism, guilt, resentment) _____

_____

_____

_____

_____

3. What is being hurt, threatened, or interfered with? (e.g., self-esteem, goals, security, personal or sexual relations)_____

_____

_____

_____

_____

_____

RECOVERY FROM OVERDEVELOPED SENSE OF RESPONSIBILITY

DESCRIPTION

Accepting the fact that we are not responsible for others allows us time to take care of ourselves. We understand that we do not have an influence on the lives of others, and thus we realize that people are responsible for their own actions. As we take responsibility for our own actions, we become aware that we must take care of our own needs and rely on our Higher Power for guidance. We find time to support and nurture ourselves, as well as others.

FEELINGS AND BEHAVIOR

1. TAKE CARE OF SELF   3. ACCEPT OUR SHORTCOMINGS
2. ENJOY LEISURE TIME

1. List specific examples of your behavior that indicate you are not taking responsibility for others. _____

_____

_____

_____

_____

_____

_____

_____

_____

_____

_____

2. What do you hope to achieve as you allow others to take responsibility for themselves and begin taking care of yourself? _____

_____

_____

_____

_____

_____

_____

_____

_____

_____

_____

SEXUALITY

DESCRIPTION

We find ourselves confused and uncertain about our sexual feelings toward others, particularly those we are close to or those with whom we desire to be emotionally intimate. We have been trained to think of our sexual feelings as unnatural, or abnormal. Because we do not share our feelings with others, we have no opportunity to develop a healthy attitude about our own sexuality. As small children, we may have explored our physical sexuality with peers and been punished for our transgressions. The message was "sex is dirty, not talked about, and is to be avoided."

Some of us saw our parents as nonsexual beings and believed we were the result of a "virgin birth." We may have been molested by a parent or close relative who was out of control because of excessive drinking or substance abuse. We are uncomfortable in our sexual role and may be sexually unsatisfied. We are inhibited from discussing sex with our partner for fear that our partner will not understand and will abandon us. If we have children, we may avoid discussions about sexuality and deny their need for sexual identity.

FEELINGS AND BEHAVIOR

1. LUST
2. INCEST
3. SEXUAL OBSESSION
4. SEDUCTIVE
5. SEXUAL IDENTITY CONFUSION
6. LOSS OF MORALITY
7. FRIGIDITY
8. IMPOTENCE

1. List specific examples of your behavior that indicate you have problems dealing with your sexuality. _____
   _____
   _____
   _____
   _____

2. What do you believe is the underlying cause of this behavior? (e.g., inadequacy, anxiety, insecurity, guilt). _____
   _____
   _____
   _____
   _____

3. What is being hurt, threatened, or interfered with? (e.g., self-esteem, goals, security, personal or sexual relations). _____
   _____
   _____
   _____
   _____

RECOVERY FROM SEXUALITY

DESCRIPTION

By relying upon the consistent love of our Higher Power, our self-worth increases. As we increase our self-love and our ability to take care of ourselves, we seek out healthy people who love and take care of themselves. We are no longer afraid of commitment and are better prepared to enter into a healthy relationship—emotionally, intellectually, and sexually. We feel more secure in sharing our feelings, strengths, and weaknesses. Our self-confidence grows and allows us to be vulnerable. We give up the need for perfection in ourselves and in others and, in so doing, open ourselves to discussion and change. We are honest about our own sexuality in discussions with our children, and we accept their need for information and sexual identity development.

FEELINGS AND BEHAVIOR

1. HONEST EXPRESSION OF FEELINGS
2. CONSIDERATION OF OUR OWN NEEDS
3. SHARE INTIMATE FEELINGS
4. SELF-CONFIDENCE
5. ACCCEPTANCE OF SEXUAL SELF

1. List specific examples of how your behavior is improving. _____

_____

_____

_____

_____

_____

_____

_____

_____

2. What do you hope to achieve as you feel more confident with your sexuality? _____

_____

_____

_____

_____

_____

_____

_____

_____

_____

CHARACTER TRAIT EXERCISE (WEAKNESSES)

Use the following characteristics to identify your actions when displaying character defects. Review what you wrote in your inventory and note the ways in which the following characteristics appear.

1. **PRIDE:** Inordinate self-esteem. Disdainful behavior or treatment.

2. **GREED** (Selfishness): Excessive or reprehensible acquisitiveness. Not having enough. Energy focused on having our way. To get our way, we injure others in the process.

3. **LUST** (Lechery): An intense desire, need, or sexual urge. Often motivated by fear of rejection.

4. **DISHONESTY** (Deceit) Disposition to defraud or deceive. Justifying our behaviors to others by explaining ourselves dishonestly.

5. **GLUTTONY** (Covetousness): One given habitually to greedy or voracious eating or drinking. Fear of rejection or worthlessness.

6. **ENVY** (Jealousy): Painful or resentful awareness of an advantage enjoyed by another, joined with a desire to possess the same advantage. Belief may be that one person is the source of one's love.

7. **LAZINESS:** Disinclined to activity or exertion; not energetic or vigorous. Fear of responsibility.

Select a character trait from your inventory (e.g., approval seeking). Describe what you discovered about the trait that caused you to slip into one or more of the characteristics listed above. (e.g., approval seeking may prompt dishonesty) ＿＿＿＿＿＿＿＿＿

＿＿＿＿＿＿＿＿＿＿＿＿＿＿＿＿＿＿＿＿＿＿＿＿＿＿＿＿＿＿＿

＿＿＿＿＿＿＿＿＿＿＿＿＿＿＿＿＿＿＿＿＿＿＿＿＿＿＿＿＿＿＿

＿＿＿＿＿＿＿＿＿＿＿＿＿＿＿＿＿＿＿＿＿＿＿＿＿＿＿＿＿＿＿

＿＿＿＿＿＿＿＿＿＿＿＿＿＿＿＿＿＿＿＿＿＿＿＿＿＿＿＿＿＿＿

＿＿＿＿＿＿＿＿＿＿＿＿＿＿＿＿＿＿＿＿＿＿＿＿＿＿＿＿＿＿＿

＿＿＿＿＿＿＿＿＿＿＿＿＿＿＿＿＿＿＿＿＿＿＿＿＿＿＿＿＿＿＿

＿＿＿＿＿＿＿＿＿＿＿＿＿＿＿＿＿＿＿＿＿＿＿＿＿＿＿＿＿＿＿

＿＿＿＿＿＿＿＿＿＿＿＿＿＿＿＿＿＿＿＿＿＿＿＿＿＿＿＿＿＿＿

＿＿＿＿＿＿＿＿＿＿＿＿＿＿＿＿＿＿＿＿＿＿＿＿＿＿＿＿＿＿＿

＿＿＿＿＿＿＿＿＿＿＿＿＿＿＿＿＿＿＿＿＿＿＿＿＿＿＿＿＿＿＿

＿＿＿＿＿＿＿＿＿＿＿＿＿＿＿＿＿＿＿＿＿＿＿＿＿＿＿＿＿＿＿

＿＿＿＿＿＿＿＿＿＿＿＿＿＿＿＿＿＿＿＿＿＿＿＿＿＿＿＿＿＿＿

＿＿＿＿＿＿＿＿＿＿＿＿＿＿＿＿＿＿＿＿＿＿＿＿＿＿＿＿＿＿＿

CHARACTER TRAIT EXERCISE (STRENGTHS)

In recovery, we replace fear with faith and deepen our trust in our Higher Power. We view ourselves as a combination of desirable and less desirable traits. We accept ourselves and all that we find within us.

1. **HUMILITY** (Modesty): Admit powerlessness and unmanageability as we accept our strengths and weaknesses.

2. **GENEROSITY** (Sharing): Feeling good about ourselves empowers us to care about the welfare and happiness of others.

3. **CONFIDENCE AND ACCEPTANCE OF SEXUAL SELF:** Feeling comfortable being sensuous, without having it lead to sexual intercourse. Clearly expressing preferences for sexual activity with partner.

4. **HONESTY:** Telling the truth, adhering to the facts, and responding to questions about our behavior with a feeling of security and self confidence.

5. **TEMPERANCE:** Moderation in activities, thoughts, or feelings. Stop using food or drink to avoid feelings or to conceal low self-esteem.

6. **AMICABLE, TRUSTFUL:** Encouragement and enthusiasm expressed toward others.

7. **ENERGETIC:** Self-starter; handle tasks without having to be told. Lively, prompt. Pay attention to work; find easier or simpler ways to do tasks.

Select a character trait from your inventory (e.g., approval seeking). Describe what you discover about the trait when you are demonstrating recovery. (e.g., tell the truth about how we feel)_____

_____

_____

_____

_____

_____

_____

_____

_____

_____

_____

_____

_____

_____

_____

_____

NOTES: _____

_____

_____

_____

_____

_____

_____

_____

_____

_____

_____

_____

_____

_____

_____

_____

_____

_____

_____

_____

_____

_____

_____

_____

_____

_____

_____

_____

_____

_____

_____

_____

_____

_____

STEP FIVE

ADMITTED TO GOD, TO OURSELVES, AND TO ANOTHER HUMAN BEING THE EXACT NATURE OF OUR WRONGS

Some of the truths of our lives were revealed in Step Four. The task of taking inventory was not easy. It demanded honesty, thoroughness, and balance. It took great courage to face the facts we discovered about ourselves by venturing into uncharted areas. If completed honestly, Step Four brought to light unresolved feelings, unhealed memories, and personal defects that have produced resentment, depression, and loss of self-worth. This process helped us confront the denial and self-deception that have been patterns in our lives.

1. How successful do you feel you were in completing your Step Four inventory? Explain.

   _____

   _____

   _____

Thoroughness in the Fourth Step helped us to see things as they really are. If we worked hard to uncover all the facts and did so thoroughly, Step Five will be more effective and rewarding. Balance in the Fourth Step inventory meant focusing on our strengths and weaknesses. Step Four helped to boost our self-esteem because we accepted all aspects of ourselves. For those who have been honest, thorough, and balanced, the writing of Step Four has been a gratifying experience. It has exposed us to many new discoveries and has provided us with a great sense of relief.

2. What part of your inventory gave you the most difficulty?_____

   _____

   _____

   _____

3. Having completed Step Four, what is your current opinion of yourself? How do you see yourself increasing your strengths and improving on your weaknesses? _____

   _____

   _____

   _____

It is important to recognize that the relationship we have with our Higher Power is the source and foundation of our courage to enter into the task ahead of us. Reliance on our Higher Power will help us become more willing to take risks. This willingness makes it possible for us to proceed with Step Five.

4. In what ways are you now experiencing fear or lack of courage in preparing your Fifth Step? _____

   _____

   _____

   _____

63

A good Fifth Step is possible after the successful completion of Step Four. We have accepted the reality of our character defects and the influence they have had on our lives. Having made a searching and fearless moral inventory, we are in a good position to complete the requirements of Step Five.

5. How will Step Five help you to recognize and deal with your own shortcomings? _____
_____
_____
_____

We will be telling our life story to three individuals—God, ourselves, and another human being. It is important to tell all that needs to be told so that we cleanse our being and are ready to move toward a deepened sense of spirituality. We may experience removal of guilt and feel like a weight has been lifted. Some of us will feel cleansed and renewed.

6. List any fears you have that need to be turned over (Step Three) before you can successfully complete Step Five._____
_____
_____
_____

7. Review your Step Four inventory to verify its completeness. What, if anything, has been omitted?_____
_____
_____
_____

Step Five is a pathway out of isolation and loneliness. It is a step toward wholeness, happiness, and a real sense of gratitude. It questions our humility. Are we truly humble in the sense that we see ourselves as one of many human beings, all as children of God? If we are humble, we will feel secure and self-accepting when admitting to God the exact nature of our wrongs. Humility will also allow us to shift the weight of the Fifth Step onto our Higher Power and experience success in working the Fifth Step.

8. In view of your former attempts to change ineffective behavior traits or patterns, how do you consider this Step essential to improvement? _____
_____
_____
_____

Step Five has three distinct parts. Admitting the exact nature of our wrongs to ourselves is the least threatening part and can be done with minimal risk. It does not provide an arena for testing our honesty or for seeing our own self-deception. Talking to ourselves holds back our ability to see ourselves in a realistic perspective. Fooling ourselves has been a pattern of our lives. Being alone with our own thoughts and feelings keeps us isolated and is limiting in nature. This isolation not only keeps others out, it keeps us in. The admission of our wrongs to ourselves prepares us for our conversation with God.

9. How has admitting your shortcomings only to yourself in the past caused you to excuse them or do nothing constructive about them?_____

_____

_____

_____

10. How has isolating yourself kept you from being honest with yourself and others?_____

_____

_____

_____

Step Five is an advancement toward ultimate surrender to a Higher Power, "Letting Go and Letting God." We must give up our desire to control the outcome. We must be willing to surrender the past and turn it over to a compassionate God who is understanding and forgiving. Admitting our wrongs to God is not for His benefit. It is an opportunity for us to realize that our Higher Power already knows us and is patiently waiting for us to confess how we still try to run the show. Trusting that our Higher Power is loving and forgiving, we become willing to admit our character defects to Him. In doing this, we experience a deepening sense of self-acceptance.

11. What method do you feel most comfortable with when admitting your wrongs to God?

_____

_____

_____

12. How can kneeling for part of your admission to God help you to experience humility?

_____

_____

_____

Nothing draws us to each other like honesty and humility. These qualities represent true humanity, which is what really attracts us to others. If we have been humble and honest with God and ourselves, completing the final stage of Step Five will be relatively easy. We need only find the right person with whom to share our wrongs.

13. Describe your experience in admitting your wrongs to God. _____

_____

_____

_____

_____

_____

14. Describe your experience in admitting your wrongs to yourself. _____
    _____
    _____
    _____

15. What life experiences helped you to understand that being honest is an important part
    of acknowledging your faults? _____
    _____
    _____
    _____

The difficult part of Step Five is facing the need to admit our wrongs to another human
being. This can be a frightening experience—to allow another person to see many parts
of us that have been hidden behind our wall of self-deception. Some of our concerns may
be that we will be laughed at or rejected for the horrors we reveal. This is a true test of
our ability and willingness to be completely honest and to accept the consequences.

16. What value do you see in admitting your faults privately to another person whom
    you respect and whom you trust to keep your confidence? _____
    _____
    _____
    _____

17. Explain any resistance you have to discussing your faults openly with another person.
    _____
    _____
    _____

Decide on a dependable person, one familiar with the Program. Trusting the person
we choose is essential to our success so that we can feel safe and unthreatened when exposing
ourselves and our behavior. Sharing will flow easily if we understand one another and accept
the limitations we all share as human beings. It is also important to recognize the unlimited
forgiveness of our Higher Power.

18. What qualities are you looking for when choosing a person with whom to share your
    Fifth Step? _____
    _____
    _____
    _____

When bringing our hidden thoughts to others, we need to do more than just be heard.
We must be ready to listen to the other person's response. The interchange can be helpful
and productive if we are willing to listen with an open mind to someone else's viewpoint.
This broadens our awareness of ourselves and gives us an opportunity to change and grow.
Feedback is vital to us as a means of completing the process of revelation. Questions asked

in a caring and understanding manner can reveal feelings and situations that we were not aware of prior to sharing our life story.

19. Why is it important to allow feedback when sharing your Fifth Step with another person? What can be gained from listening to the other person's viewpoint?_____

_____

_____

_____

When preparing for the Fifth Step, either as the participant or as the listener, the following suggestions are helpful:
   A.   Be aware of the vulnerability of the participant.
   B.   Allow sufficient time to complete each thought, but stay focused on the subject. Discourage unnecessary explanations.
   C.   Minimize distractions. Telephone calls, children, visitors, and extraneous noises can interfere with the flow of concentration.
   D.   Prayer may prove useful—before, during, and after.
   E.   Listen carefully. Ask questions if necessary so that the information will be understood by both parties.
   F.   Remember that Step Five asks only that we admit the exact nature of our wrongs. It is not necessary to discuss how changes are going to be made.
   G.   Be supportive and acknowledge the person for the effort exerted in completing the Step.
   H.   When completed, each may share feelings about the experience and toward the other person.

Upon completion of Step Five, we may have expectations about where we should be in our process of recovery. How we feel is beside the point. We may not feel any differently than we did before. The real test of our Fifth Step admission is how willing we are to change our ways.

20. What was revealed to you following your Fifth Step with God, yourself, and another human being? _____

_____

_____

_____

21. Briefly review Steps One through Four and identify anything you may have omitted that was brought to light as a result of sharing your life story with another person. ____

_____

_____

_____

_____

_____

We realize that we are not always in control of things. Longstanding habits may have weakened our will to such an extent that it is extremely difficult to break our behavior patterns. We need to be realistic and understand that admitting the exact nature of our wrongs is not insurance against future lapses. We can expect to have lapses and still know that our relationship with our Higher Power will help us to face and overcome them.

22. Describe your feelings after taking Step Five. Did you feel closer to your fellows, more a part of the human race? _____

_____

_____

_____

23. Describe any areas about which you felt uncomfortable while sharing. _____

_____

_____

_____

24. Did you experience an increased level of peace and serenity, or was there sadness, anxiety, etc.? Explain. _____

_____

_____

_____

It is not our intentions that matter. If we sincerely desire to change our ways, all God asks is that we pick ourselves up one more time than we fall. The end result of making our admission is not "results" so much as an experience of the reality of God's love.

25. In what ways did Step Five bring you closer to God and help you to gain a better opinion of yourself? _____

_____

_____

_____

NOTES: _____

_____

_____

_____

_____

_____

_____

_____

STEP SIX

WERE ENTIRELY READY TO HAVE GOD REMOVE ALL THESE DEFECTS OF CHARACTER

Our success in working Steps One through Five is an indication of our readiness to complete Step Six. Steps One and Two prepared us for Step Three, at which time we made a decision to turn our will and our lives over to the care of God as we understood Him. Steps Four and Five helped us to uncover our defects of character. We faced them courageously and shared them with God, ourselves, and another human being. We have acknowledged our shortcomings without guilt because we have learned that blaming and punishing ourselves stunts our growth. The guilt feelings are natural, but to cling to them will keep us at a standstill. Step Six is another opportunity to turn our will over. The trust we have developed in, and our current feelings toward, our Higher Power is an encouraging prospect for having our character defects removed.

1. List those areas in your life about which you still have guilt feelings. _____
    _____
    _____
    _____

2. Are you consciously aware of being ready to have God remove your character defects? List some of the changes you see in yourself as a result of being ready. _____
    _____
    _____
    _____

The character traits we have identified as defects are deeply ingrained patterns of behavior. They are tools we have acquired and used for survival in our daily lives. As we become aware of these defects and accept them, we can deal with them from a position of strength with the help of our Higher Power. Sharing our awareness of our defects honestly with our Higher Power and trusting that He will help us remove them is the foundation of our strength and hope.

3. What anxieties are present when you consider the idea of having your "survival tools" removed? _____
    _____
    _____
    _____

4. What feelings surface when you think of surrendering to your Higher Power and trusting that He will remove your defects? _____
    _____
    _____
    _____

In our culture, self-will is a highly valued trait. We are taught from an early age that we should try to improve ourselves. Our parents, teachers, and employers have told us that it is our duty to them and to God that we work on our own defects. As a result, we use our self-will to accumulate and demonstrate success. It is a rare person who attributes his or her success to the existence of a Higher Power and surrenders to Him.

5. How are you relating with your Higher Power at this point in working the Steps? _____

_____

_____

_____

6. How much of your progress do you attribute to your relationship with your Higher Power? _____

_____

_____

_____

7. What is the touchstone (role model or ideal) you use to remind you of true surrender?

_____

_____

_____

We are often comfortable with some of our defects. They have been familiar tools to us. The thought of having them removed can be threatening to our security. As difficult as it may seem, we must be willing to let go of these defects in order to become entirely ready to have God remove them. Being entirely ready requires a dedication like that illustrated in preparing for a race, learning to speak in front of an audience, or developing skills as an artist. Certain tasks must be performed in order to succeed.

8. Identify any character defects you are not entirely ready to have removed. Explain briefly your attachment to these defects. _____

_____

_____

_____

9. List ways that indicate you are willing to accept the notion that God loves you just the way you are, defects and all. _____

_____

_____

_____

Preparing to be entirely ready to have God remove our defects of character is accomplished through the training we have undergone in the first Five Steps. We have inadvertently begun to experience confidence in the ongoing process of working and living the Steps one day at a time. Being entirely ready implies trust, faith, and belief that the one we are going to ask will fulfill our request.

10. In what ways have the first Five Steps helped you to prepare for Step Six? _____
_____
_____
_____

11. What is your current level of confidence in working the Steps as a means of improving the quality of your life? _____
_____
_____
_____

An important ingredient in preparing for Step Six is humility. We must relinquish our egos, truly seek God's will for us. Our trust in God tells us that He will remove only the defects that are necessary. The way to learn what God has in mind for us is to be ready for God to remove our desire for things that are not good for us.

12. How do you see humility as necessary for letting go and allowing God to remove your defects? _____
_____
_____
_____

The task of removing all of our character defects is more than we can handle, we are not able to do it alone. Step Six does not say we have to do the removing. All we have to do is allow it to happen, let go. It is not an action step that we actually take. It is a state of being that takes us. One day we realize that we no longer have any qualms about letting God remove any and all of our character defects as He sees fit. This we do by faithfully working the Program, day by day, whether we feel like we're making progress or not.

13. Give an example of how you are inspired by the prospect of having God remove your character defects. _____
_____
_____
_____

14. What experiences have you had that indicate you are making progress toward allowing God to remove your defects? _____
_____
_____
_____

For some of the more deeply rooted defects, we may find it necessary to become a detached observer. By becoming an observer of our behavior and of the behavior of others, we notice how we act or react in various situations. When we see ourselves thinking negatively or doing something that is not constructive, we can make a note of it and ask for help from our Higher Power. By doing this, the task will become much easier.

15. What character defects are going to be the most difficult to give up? _____

_____

_____

_____

16. Why are these defects so important, and what do you fear as a result of having them removed?

_____

_____

_____

Some people reach a state of preparedness quickly and are ready to have God remove all of their character defects. For most of us, the process is slow and gradual. When we cling to old habits and unproductive ways of thinking, we block the process of change and the flow of inspiration. One way to use God's help is to allow solutions to come to us by turning to our Higher Power. This can be done by saying the Serenity Prayer as often as necessary.

17. How are the Program tools (slogans, prayers, writing) you use in your daily life helping you with Step Six? _____

_____

_____

_____

18. What is the most effective means by which you turn to your Higher Power for guidance? (e.g., prayer, meetings)_____

_____

_____

_____

It may be beneficial to analyze our communication with God. The following statements are examples of the distinction between asking and admitting. "Dear God, I want to be more patient" is making a demand and telling God what we want. "Dear God, I am impatient" is presenting the truth about ourselves. This allows God to make the decision for us based on our admission.

19. List examples of your prayers that show you are making demands on God, rather than asking for His will._____

_____

_____

_____

As we live the principles of the Program in our daily lives, we gradually and unconsciously become ready to have our defects of character removed. What sometimes happens is that we are not aware of being ready to have our defects removed or of asking God to remove them. The first awareness we have is that we are different somehow. We have changed. Often the change is noticed by others before we become aware of it ourselves. The approval-seeking person begins to function more adequately; the control addict becomes warmer and more relaxed; the super-responsible individual is no longer victimizing himself by doing for others what they can do for themselves. People who work the Program as an integral part of their lives become calmer, more serene, and wear genuine smiles. Much of the work we do in the Program is done without conscious action on our part.

20. What changes have occurred in your life that most effectively show your behavior is improving? _____

_____

_____

_____

21. What parts of **THE PROBLEM** (See Step One) do you feel you are overcoming or coming to terms with? _____

_____

_____

_____

22. What parts of **THE PROBLEM** (See Step One) do you feel are still actively causing you discomfort? _____

_____

_____

_____

There is a radiant, confident personality in each of us, hidden under a shroud of confusion, uncertainty, and defects. If someone were to ask whether we wanted to be freed from our character defects, there could only be one answer—that we are entirely ready to have God remove them.

23. Describe your understanding of the words "entirely ready." What do they mean in relation to your complete surrender to God's will? _____

_____

_____

_____

_____

The Twelve Steps—A Way Out

NOTES:

STEP SEVEN

HUMBLY ASKED HIM TO REMOVE OUR SHORTCOMINGS

Attainment of greater humility is the foundation principle of the ACA Twelve Step Program. It is through humility that we reach the goals as outlined in the Steps. The basic ingredient in humility as it applies to the program is a desire to seek and do God's will.

1. What is your definition of humility? _____
   _____
   _____
   _____

In working and living Steps One and Two, a degree of humility was necessary when we admitted our powerlessness and came to believe that a Power greater than ourselves could restore us to sanity. In Step Three, humility allowed us to turn our will and our lives over to the care of God as we understood Him. Without humility, Steps Four and Five would be extremely difficult. In Step Six, our being ready to have our defects removed was in direct proportion to the degree of our humility.

2. How have you practiced humility while working the Steps? _____
   _____
   _____
   _____

The entire emphasis in Step Seven is humility. This is the point at which we change our attitude and move from being self-centered to self-less. This produces harmony with God and other people. As we grow in the Program, we see humility as being absolutely necessary for survival. Humility is simply the growing awareness that "Of myself I am nothing, the Father doeth the work." Only by a deepening awareness of this can we humbly ask God to remove our shortcomings.

3. Give examples of how being humble is helping you to focus less on yourself and more on your Higher Power. _____
   _____
   _____
   _____

We desire humility because we realize that it is the only way to achieve the peace, serenity, and happiness we seek. If we desire to be a maturing, growing, useful, joyous person, we will have to develop an inner calm, even in a turbulent, insane world. To achieve this inner calm, we must develop the ability to accept things as they are when we cannot change them and to ask God for the courage to change the things we can.

4. Describe a recent event that prompted you to use the Serenity Prayer in order to help you to achieve inner calm. _____
   _____

_____

_____

Step Seven implies removal of all our shortcomings. It is important that we deal with them individually, preferably with the easiest ones first to build confidence in our progress. Our commitment to doing the footwork one day at a time supports the idea that progress will come at a comfortable pace with God's help. If we ask God to remove a character defect and it is not removed, we do not need to be discouraged or angry. We need to be patient and realize that we have more work to do. We may not be entirely ready to have it removed, or we may not have humbly asked God.

5. What does "Humbly asked Him to remove our shortcomings" mean to you? _____

    _____

    _____

    _____

6. Are you ready to have all your shortcomings removed, or do you have favorites you feel justified in keeping? Explain. _____

    _____

    _____

    _____

In preparing to have our defects removed, we must demonstrate our complete willingness on an ongoing basis. We must cooperate. We cannot expect our shortcomings to be removed if we continue to behave the way we did before and simply wait for God to do all the work. Even though we have asked, it is important to be aware of any tendencies to repeat old behavior. Anytime we become aware of the "old defects" at work, being gentle with ourselves at that moment is very important. God loves us however we are, and it is an opportunity for us to love ourselves. This is simply an indication that some part of us still wants to hang on, that we are learning to accept God's will, but that we are not yet humble enough to willingly let go.

7. How do you see yourself behaving in the "old" manner? _____

    _____

    _____

    _____

8. What are your fears surrounding the idea of no longer having certain familiar behaviors?

    _____

    _____

    _____

Being open to the wisdom and guidance of our Higher Power is vital at this time. When meditating on the recurrence of behaviors that we consider "immature," it is wise to remind ourselves that our inner-child is "unmatured." If we are willing to grow spiritually and emotionally, we will see progress. Any improvement is cause for gratitude and joy.

We need to remember that this process of spiritual development is lifelong, yet we practice it one day at a time or one minute at a time if necessary.

9. Where do you see yourself as being "unmatured?" _____

   _____

   _____

   _____

10. How can you acknowledge the progress you have made in handling situations maturely?

    _____

    _____

    _____

No matter how hard we try, we can never hope to eliminate all our character defects, in spite of all the praying we do for guidance. Achieving sainthood is not part of this program. We simply do the best we can. We are not expected to fit any image at all. We are only required to humbly ask that our shortcomings be removed.

11. In what ways have you become more patient with yourself as a result of working the

    Program? _____

    _____

    _____

    _____

Humbly asking God to remove our shortcomings is a true means of surrender and may be difficult for some of us. As M. Scott Peck pointed out in his book, *The Road Less Traveled*, depression often accompanies the process of releasing. "There are many factors that can interfere with the giving-up process and, therefore, prolong a normal, healthy depression into a chronic pathologic depression. Of all the possible factors, one of the most common and potent is a pattern of experiences in childhood wherein parents or fate, unresponsive to the needs of the child, took away 'things' from the child before he or she was psychologically ready to give them up or strong enough to truly accept their loss. Such a pattern of experience in childhood sensitizes the child to the experience of loss and creates a tendency far stronger than that found in more fortunate individuals to cling to 'things' and seek to avoid the pain of loss or giving up. For this reason, although all pathologic depressions involve some blockage in the giving-up process, I believe there is a type of chronic neurotic depression that has as its central root a traumatic injury to the individual's basic capacity to give up anything . . ."[2] Much of the work done in this Workbook is to heal the pain of the inner-child.

12. What "things" were taken away from you as a child before you were ready to give

    them up? _____

    _____

    _____

    _____

13.   How has this contributed to your current condition? _____

_____

_____

_____

Humbly asking a child to set the table for dinner, then impatiently doing it yourself can be likened to humbly asking God to remove your shortcomings, then insisting on removing them yourself. In neither case are you humbly asking for anything to be done. No one can truly take credit for removing any of their character defects. If we expect any credit, we are doomed to failure. Sudden changes can and do happen, but we cannot expect them or direct them. God causes them when we are ready for them. When we humbly ask God to do the removing, it becomes His responsibility and we cannot accept credit or blame for what follows.

14.   What is your reaction to the idea that God will not remove all your character defects?

_____

_____

_____

15.   What is your reaction to the idea that they cannot be removed until you are ready? _____

_____

_____

_____

The items that remain in our inventory after this process is completed must belong there. It is an opportunity for us to take these remaining "defects" and allow God to turn them into positive traits. With God's help, this can be a rewarding and exciting experience. Natural leaders may be left with a quest for power but with no desire to misuse it. Natural lovers will be left with exquisite sensuality but with enough consideration not to hurt anyone with it. Those who are meant to be materially wealthy will be, but without greed and possessiveness.

16.   What personal qualities remain from your inventory that have the potential of being

assets rather than liabilities? _____

_____

_____

_____

In order to work the Program successfully, we must practice The Steps on a daily basis until it becomes a routine. In this way, we will eventually be capable of breaking the bonds of our old and unhealthy habits and behaviors. We will begin to trust the thoughts and feelings that show up as a result of our conscious contact with God. We will come to know that the guidance we receive from our Higher Power is always available; all we need to do is listen and act without fear.

SEVENTH STEP PRAYER

"My Creator, I am now willing that you should have all of me, good and bad. I pray that you now remove from me every single defect of character which stands in your way of my usefulness to you and my fellow. Grant me the strength, as I go out from here, to do your bidding. Amen."[3]

Big Book (A.A.)

SERENITY PRAYER

"God, grant me the serenity
to accept the things I cannot change,
the courage to change the things I can,
and the wisdom to know the difference."

2. M. Scott Peck, M.D., *The Road Less Traveled*, (New York: Simon and Schuster, Inc.), p. 70.
3. Alcoholics Anonymous, Alcoholics Anonymous World Services, Inc. (New York), p.76.

SERENITY PRAYER EXERCISE

The following examples are intended to help you in using the Serenity Prayer as part of your ongoing recovery process. It is a tool that can be used daily when seeking God's help. The exercise gives you an opportunity to take a situation through the prayer.

God, grant me the serenity to accept the things I cannot change .... like the way _____ ignores me, especially when I want praise.

the courage to change the things I can ..... especially my own character defects and feelings toward myself for never having enough approval from people I look up to.

and the wisdom to know the difference ..... between the lasting satisfaction of reparenting myself with approval and the temporary satisfaction of depending on _____ for it.

God, grant me the serenity to accept the things I cannot change .... like the way my childhood was.

the courage to change the things I can ..... especially my own victimized feelings about my childhood.

and the wisdom to know the difference ..... between staying in a victim role and continually turning those years over to my Higher Power.

God, grant me the serenity to accept the things I cannot change .... like my father's disease of alcoholism.

the courage to change the things I can ..... especially my feelings of abandonment, anger, isolation.

and the wisdom to know the difference ..... between my father's love being unavailable to me and my Higher Power which is always with me.

Select a specific situation or condition in your life that is currently a source of resentment, fear, sadness, or anger. It may involve relationships (family, work, or sexual), work environment, health, or self-esteem.

GOD, GRANT ME THE SERENITY TO ACCEPT THE THINGS I CANNOT CHANGE

1. State the condition or experience you are aware of that you cannot change. (e.g., childhood, partner's behavior, employment conditions, parents' behavior) _____

    _____

    _____

    _____

    _____

    _____

THE COURAGE TO CHANGE THE THINGS I CAN

2. Indicate the specific condition or situation where you believe change is possible. _____

    _____

    _____

    _____

    _____

    _____

AND THE WISDOM TO KNOW THE DIFFERENCE

3. Identify your understanding and acceptance of what you can and cannot change. (e.g., frozen feelings vs. flowing feelings; anger vs. peace) _____

    _____

    _____

    _____

    _____

    _____

4. List any insights gained from this exercise. _____

    _____

    _____

    _____

    _____

    _____

    _____

    _____

    _____

NOTES: _____

_____

_____

_____

_____

_____

_____

_____

_____

_____

_____

_____

_____

_____

_____

_____

_____

_____

_____

_____

_____

_____

_____

_____

_____

_____

_____

_____

_____

_____

_____

_____

STEP EIGHT

MADE A LIST OF ALL PERSONS WE HAD HARMED, AND BECAME WILLING TO MAKE AMENDS TO THEM ALL

Step Eight is the beginning of the end of our isolation from our fellows and from God. Relationships are what Step Eight and Nine are all about—our relationships with other people, with ourselves, and with our Higher Power. In this step, we must show a desire and willingness to write down each of our past misdeeds, the dates, and the names of those people involved. We cannot remake the present until we undo the past. This is done gradually by gently loving ourselves as we mature and by allowing our inner child to grow up.

1. How will Step Eight improve your relationship with others? _____
   _____
   _____
   _____

The first Seven Steps are "personal" in that they are concerned with an examination of our behavior patterns and are intended to make us aware of our personal experiences. By the time we reach this point in recovery, we are beginning to see how important it is for us to let go of the past with its painful and sometimes pleasurable memories. Through these changes in our awareness, we learn to live each day in harmony with ourselves and others. Releasing the past opens the path to a new life for us, a life based on living one day at a time.

2. List three personal experiences that require making amends. _____
   _____
   _____
   _____

3. How will making amends release the past? _____
   _____
   _____
   _____

In order to find enjoyment in recovery, it is important that we develop the ability to overcome guilt, shame, resentment, low self-worth, and fear of other people. To accomplish this may seem like an awesome task since we have probably tried to do it before. This time, however, we have the opportunity to restore our personal integrity and self-authority by working the Steps. We can trust in the process because it has worked miracles for millions of people.

4. How will making amends help remove your guilt, shame, and resentments? _____
   _____
   _____
   _____

5. What do you hope to achieve by making amends? _____
_____
_____
_____

The first part of Step Eight specifically states that we make a list of those we have harmed. When making the list, many of us may hit a solid obstacle. It can be a severe shock to realize that we must make a face-to-face admission of our past wrongs to those we have harmed. It was embarrassing enough to admit them to ourselves, to God, and to another human being in Step Five. In Step Nine, we actually have to visit or write the people concerned.

6. What is your interpretation of "harmed?" List the actions or experiences you believe are harmful to yourself or to others. _____
_____
_____
_____

Those who have successfully worked the first Five Steps are usually aware of those they have harmed by the time they reach Step Eight. You may discover that the person you have harmed most is yourself. Sometimes we realize that we have become our own worst enemy, and our resentment against ourselves manifests itself in the form of excessive self-blame, guilt, and sometimes shame. Guilt is an appropriate response to regrets over actions in conflict with our personal values. Shame is excessive guilt and may cause us to view ourselves as bad or worthless, which is unhealthy.

7. Are you willing to forgive yourself for the things you have done to cause harm or injury to others? List the major ways in which you have harmed yourself. _____
_____
_____
_____

When starting Step Eight, make a list of the people you feel uncomfortable with. Just make a list. Don't worry about the details. Making the list enables us to go where our mind takes us. Our list may start with family members, business associates, friends, creditors, and neighbors. Its length is not important, yet it may reveal a somewhat unrealistic view of the power of our personal influence. Step Eight is another exercise in preparation for the ongoing process of healing that this Program offers. The powerful elixir of honesty is what makes the healing take place.

8. Examine the list of people you have harmed. Identify the things you have done that caused physical, mental, or spiritual harm to each person. _____
_____
_____
_____

9. Which people on your list do you feel the greatest need to make amends with? _____

_____

_____

_____

In order to complete this Step, we must be willing to face the facts and make amends. We must be ready to willingly accept the consequences and take whatever measures are necessary to make restitution. This may be difficult for some of us because it means fully and completely acknowledging our part of every dispute in which harm has come to someone as a result of our action or inaction. We need to do this, regardless of cause, no matter how justified we may have felt. Only by expressing genuine regret for our own part in the dispute can we complete our housecleaning. This housecleaning is necessary for us to develop spiritually and to achieve the peace and serenity we desire.

10. Are you willing to go to any length to make the amends? Identify any reluctance and describe your feelings toward the person. _____

_____

_____

_____

Forgiveness is the next key factor in completing Step Eight. We must be willing to forgive ourselves as well as those who we feel have caused us harm. This takes a great deal of humility on our part. We have already become aware that resentments and grudges are luxuries we cannot afford. They not only destroy our serenity and sanity, but they are more harmful to us than to the person we resent. A resentment or grudge is like an open sore eating away at our insides, making us grouchy, bitter, ill-tempered, and unable to concentrate on growth because our energy is spent on our grudge or resentment.

11. In the process of preparing to make amends, have you felt a sense of forgiveness surfacing? If so, what does it feel like? _____

_____

_____

_____

12. How are resentments and grudges interfering with your willingness to make amends?

_____

_____

_____

The most effective means of overcoming resentment is forgiveness of ourselves and of others. Forgiveness of others begins when we become aware of our own contribution to the difficulties in our relationships. Looking at ourselves helps us become willing to release our anger and our condemnation of others. Through acceptance, forgiveness, and turning it over to our Higher Power, we will be able to rid ourselves of these grudges and resentments. When we understand the damage we have done, we need to make amends and reduce our likelihood of repeating this pattern of behavior. If we do not forgive ourselves, we cannot forgive others. If we do not forgive others, we cannot make amends with dignity, self-respect, and humility. Amends without forgiveness can lead us into a new argument, or dispute. Our willingness to make amends must stem from a true desire for forgiveness.

13. What part is your Higher Power playing in your preparation for making amends?_____

_____

_____

_____

14. Why is forgiveness of yourself such a key factor in completing this Step?_____

_____

_____

_____

When looking back at those we have harmed, we see how our character defects have played a major part in sabotaging ourselves and others. The following are examples of this behavior:

A. When we became angry, we often harmed ourselves more than we did others.
B. When confronted with an issue about which we felt guilt and were in denial, we lashed out at the other person rather than looking at ourselves.
C. Frustrated by our lack of control, we behaved badly and intimidated those around us.
D. Our fear of abandonment sometimes destroyed relationships because we did not allow the other person to be himself; rather, we smothered him in an effort to maintain the relationship.

15. What are the major character defects that caused injury to yourself or to others? _____

_____

_____

_____

Humility can help us see each human being as having an equal right to be here and to live as happily as we do. This does not mean we have to agree with everyone about everything, but it does mean we can stop hating people for what they have done and stop resenting them because their views are different from ours. Our own sanity will be preserved, and our serenity greatly enhanced, if we can forgive and even love our enemies rather than hate them or wish them harm.

16. Explain how you see humility as necessary to complete Step Eight successfully. _____

_____

_____

_____

As we proceed through the Steps, we do indeed learn to forgive, like, and love the enemy within us. As we learn to understand our inner enemy and accept him, our spiritual growth will advance at a rapid pace. As we forgive our outer enemies, they become less enemies and, in some cases, become close friends.

17. How do you see forgiveness of your inner and outer "enemy" as contributing to your acceptance of yourself and others? _____

_____

_____

_____

If we are willing to make amends and to face our past, we become more tolerant and forgiving, less rigid and judgmental. We will begin to realize that our Higher Power is doing for us what we could not do for ourselves. At this point, we are beginning to experience real changes in our viewpoints, attitudes, and beliefs, and we are becoming ready and willing to participate in the process of reconciliation. Now we are ready to move on to Step Nine and actually make the amends we have found necessary.

18. List examples in which your changing viewpoints and attitudes allow healthy relationships to develop. _____

_____

_____

_____

AMENDS LIST EXERCISE

Following are three main categories in which we may have caused harm and for which we must be willing to make amends.

MATERIAL WRONGS: Your actions affecting an individual in a tangible way, such as one of the following:

1. Money—borrowing or spending extravagance; stinginess; spending in an attempt to buy friendship or love; withholding money in order to gratify yourself.
2. Contracts—entering into an agreement that is legally enforceable, then not abiding by the terms, or simply cheating (e.g., a business transaction that is to provide products or services—agreeing to repay loans or make payments on time).
3. Person or Property—any injury or damage as a result of your action.
4. Personal Abuse—physical or sexual.

MORAL WRONGS: Dealing with what is right and wrong in behavior as well as in moral duty and/or obligation. Also including the questions of rightness, fairness, or equity. The principal issue is involving others in your wrongdoing:

1. Setting a bad example for children, friends, or anyone who looked to you for guidance.
2. Excessive preoccupation with selfish pursuits and using justification as your way to deny your actions. This caused you to be totally unaware of the needs of others. (e.g., preoccupation resulted in lost caring for, or attention to, children or relationship partner. Another example would be obsession with an addictive partner, possibly causing job ineffectiveness.)
3. Being forgetful of special occasions (e.g., birthdays and holidays pass unnoticed).
4. Moral harms (e.g., sexual infidelity, broken promises, verbal abuse, lack of trust, unkind criticism, lying).

SPIRITUAL WRONGS: Principally, "acts of omission" that are the neglect of obligations to God, to yourself, to family, and to community.

1. Making no effort to fulfill your obligations and showing a lack of gratitude toward others who have stepped in for you. (e.g., family and children, work tasks).
2. Avoiding self-development (e.g., health, education, recreation, creativity).
3. Being inattentive to others in your life by showing a lack of encouragement to them.

1. List six people who come to mind as being someone whom you have harmed.

   a. _____   c. _____

   b. _____   d. _____

   e. _____   f. _____

2. Identify how you harmed them. The categories listed will enable you to be very specific. (e.g., moral, unkind criticism.)

   a. _____

   b. _____

   c. _____

   d. _____

   e. _____

   f. _____

3. Select the person to whom you have caused the most harm. Answer the following questions using the person selected.

   NAME:_____   **HARM:**_____

   a. **FACTS**—What is the reason for making the amends? _____
   _____
   _____

   b. **FEARS**—What is your resistance to making the amends? _____
   _____
   _____

   c. **FEELINGS**—What are your feelings about making the amends? _____
   _____
   _____

   d. **DEFECTS**—What character trait was activated in your relationship with this person?
   _____
   _____

   e. **FORGIVENESS**—Are you willing to ask for forgiveness and face the consequences? Explain why._____
   _____
   _____

   f. **AMENDS**—When and how do you plan to make amends?_____
   _____
   _____

NOTES: _____

STEP NINE

MADE DIRECT AMENDS TO SUCH PEOPLE WHEREVER POSSIBLE, EXCEPT WHEN TO DO SO WOULD INJURE THEM OR OTHERS

Step Nine is another action step and again requires that we demonstrate a willingness to confront issues of our past, which may have been dormant for a long time. This Step clearly requires courage and a renewed understanding of our intention to free ourselves from the guilt we may feel for any hurt done to others. The benefits to us are certainly worth taking the risk of making amends.

1. What does "making *direct* amends" mean to you? _____

   _____

   _____

   _____

2. Do you understand that there is no need to review each matter to see who is at fault?

   Explain. _____

   _____

   _____

   _____

Engaging in this process of forgiveness is like having spiritual surgery performed on us. The distant memories, which may still be painful and linger in our minds, can encumber us. They diminish our vitality and joy for living. Making amends somehow seems to make many of these memories simply disappear. Being attached to someone in our memory as a result of an uncomfortable experience and, then, making amends with that person, can be likened to the release of a butterfly trapped in the hands of a curious child. Letting go allows both to explore and move about in their own independent and natural state. It also allows for a new relationship to emerge.

3. How do you see forgiveness as setting you free and healing your painful memories? _____

   _____

   _____

   _____

Good judgment, a careful sense of timing, courage, and prudence are qualities that we will need when taking Step Nine. It is wise to reflect upon the intended amends for a while. Our objective is not to buy our peace of mind at the expense of others. Forethought will prepare us for the appropriate time and deter us from causing any further harm. The process may include seeking guidance from a trusted friend as well as humbly asking our Higher Power for guidance, support, and the willingness to do whatever is necessary.

4. What is the importance of reflecting on your amends prior to making them? _____

   _____

   _____

   _____

Step Nine requires that direct amends be made wherever possible. We must be careful not to procrastinate by telling ourselves the time is not right. We may be tempted to skip the more humiliating and dreaded meetings or to find excuses to dodge the issues entirely. We must be sure that we are not delaying because of fear. Fear is lack of courage, and courage is an important part of this Step. The readiness to accept the full consequences of our past and, at the same time, take responsibility for the well-being of others is the very spirit of Step Nine.

5. How can you get the strength, support, and courage from a supportive and loving friend to make these direct amends? _____

_____

_____

_____

6. Before you start making amends, how will you make sure there is no lingering residue of resentment or self-righteousness left in you to prevent your amends from being meaningful? _____

_____

_____

_____

Amends will be possible with almost everyone, even those who may not be aware of what we have done to them. In every word or action that violates the Golden Rule, "Do unto others as we would have them do unto us," there are amends to make. If someone is unable to accept a restitution, their part of the problem will have to remain unresolved, and our using the Serenity Prayer will be helpful for our own peace of mind.

7. Describe how you will use prayer and meditation before making *direct* amends. _____

_____

_____

_____

When looking at making amends, we see that Step Nine has two distinct parts:

"MADE DIRECT AMENDS TO SUCH PEOPLE WHEREVER POSSIBLE,"

People who need to be dealt with as soon as possible and are readily accessible.

These people include family members, employees or employers, or creditors to whom we owe financial amends. They may include friends as well as enemies. It is harder to go to an enemy than to a friend, but we will find it much more beneficial to us. When we are ready to face the consequences of our past, we will be able to go to them, admit the damage we have done, and make our apologies. The generous response of most people to such sincerity will often astonish us. Even our severest and most justified critics will frequently meet us more than halfway on the first attempt.

8. What people on your amends list fall into this category? _____
    _____
    _____
    _____

9. Examine whether complete disclosure will seriously harm anyone to whom you are making amends. _____
    _____
    _____
    _____

Situations whose very nature will never allow us to make direct personal contact.

This may involve people who are no longer a part of our lives or who have died. In these cases, indirect amends can satisfy our need to make things right. We can make indirect amends through prayer or by writing a letter, as if we are actually communicating with the person. Indirect amends can also be made by doing a kindness for someone else's child or parent when we no longer have any responsibility for caring for the person. We can make amends to our adult children by respecting them as adults, by maintaining our own recovery, and by being healthy and reasonably happy adults ourselves.

10. What people on your amends list fall into this category? _____
    _____
    _____
    _____

11. Examine whether complete disclosure will seriously harm anyone to whom you are making amends. _____
    _____
    _____
    _____

"EXCEPT WHEN TO DO SO WOULD INJURE THEM OR OTHERS."

People to whom we can only make partial restitution because complete disclosure could cause harm to them or others.

These people may include our spouses, ex-partners, former business associates, or friends. We must analyze the harm that could come to them if complete amends were made. This is especially true in cases where infidelity is present in a marriage. Amends in this area can cause irreparable damage to all parties concerned. Even in cases where the matter can be discussed, we should avoid harming third parties. It does not lighten our burden when we make the crosses of others harder to bear. Amends for unfaithfulness can be made indirectly by a change in behavior, by concentrating more sincere affection and attention on the one who has been deceived.

12. What people on your amends list fall into this category? _____
_____
_____
_____

13. Examine whether complete disclosure will seriously harm anyone to whom you are making amends. _____
_____
_____
_____

In cases involving serious consequences, such as potential loss of employment, imprisonment, or other harm to one's family, each one of us has to make the decision carefully. We should not be deterred from making amends by fear for ourselves but only by the real possibility of injury to others. If we choose to delay making amends out of fear, we will be the ones to suffer in the end. We will delay our growth, experience regression, become more emotionally ill, and possibly return to our prior insane behavior.

14. What people on your amends list fall into this category? _____
_____
_____
_____

15. Examine whether complete disclosure will seriously harm anyone to whom you are making amends. _____
_____
_____
_____

Situations where action should be deferred.

In these areas, it can be helpful to seek other counsel when we assess our judgment of the situation. It is seldom wise to approach an individual who still smarts from the injustices we have done. In situations where our own hurts are still deeply imbedded, patience might prove to be wise. We can know that amends must be made eventually, but our timing is important so that we can gain and grow from the experience.

16. What people on your amends list fall into this category? _____
_____
_____
_____
_____

17. Examine whether complete disclosure will seriously harm anyone to whom you are making amends. _____

_____

_____

_____

When you actually start the process of making amends, be careful not to confuse apologies with amends. Apologies are sometimes called for, but apologies are not amends. We may discover in apologizing that we explain excessively, and this is not as effective as simply changing. Amends are made by acting differently. We can apologize a hundred times for being late for work, but this will not "mend" the tardiness. Appearing at work on time is a change in behavior, and thus becomes an amend.

18. List two examples of your distinguishing apologies from amends. _____

_____

_____

_____

Occasional emotional or spiritual relapses, or "slips," are to be expected and need to be dealt with in a timely manner. When these relapses occur, we must accept them as signals that we are forgetting something. Perhaps we have taken part of our will back from our Higher Power and need to go back to Step Three; or possibly we have eliminated something from our inventory and must go back to Step Four; or we may have a character defect that we are not willing to let go of and must return to Step Six.

19. Give examples of recent "slips" and how you dealt with them. _____

_____

_____

_____

20. What character defects caused the "slips?"_____

_____

_____

_____

In reality, the entire Twelve Step Program is one of constant repetition and gradual improvement. Most of us need to go over the Steps regularly throughout our lifetime. After the first time, the Steps do not need to be repeated in order. As we grow spiritually, we will be able to rely on them as one of the major factors in our journey toward recovery and a spiritual awakening.

21. What hesitancy do you have in working the Steps as a lifetime process?_____

_____

_____

_____

In repairing the damage we have done to others, we will also be overhauling our own lives. If we do it thoroughly, we can find ourselves returned to an amazingly peaceful state without hatred, guilt, or resentment. We will feel a glow of satisfaction in knowing we have honestly done everything we can to pay off every material, moral, and spiritual debt we owe to our fellow human beings.

22. Did you have any difficulty performing this process? If you did have resistance, how were you able to overcome it? _____

_____

_____

_____

The importance of Step Nine is obvious. It finally gives us the chance to eradicate past concerns and to start living in the present. We have taken the opportunity to balance good with evil, and it will make us feel good about ourselves. As difficult as it may have been to make amends and to replace our misery with happiness, the joy we try to give will not measure up to the pleasure this Step gives us.

23. In what way do you see that Step Five and Step Nine are exacting Steps and are important to your recovery? _____

_____

_____

_____

We are now in a place to rebuild self-esteem freely, to achieve unity with self and others, to increase self-acceptance and self-respect, and to be in harmony with God and with our own personal world.

24. Referring to your amends lists, estimate a reasonable amount of time in which the direct amends can be completed. _____

_____

_____

_____

NOTES: _____

_____

_____

_____

_____

_____

_____

_____

AMENDS TO OTHERS EXERCISE

Following is a summary of ideas and procedures that individuals have found useful in preparing for their Step Nine amends and in making the amends.

ATTITUDE
    A.   Be willing to love and forgive yourself and the person to whom the amends are made.

    B.   Know what you want to say and be careful not to blame the person in your communication.

    C.   Take responsibility for what you are going to say.

    D.   Be willing to accept the outcome.

    E.   Don't expect a particular response from the other person.

    F.   Be willing to turn it over to God.

PREPARATION
    A.   Devote time to prayer and meditation. If you are angry or upset, delay the amend and do more Step Four inventory work.

    B.   Keep it simple. Details and explanations aren't necessary.

    C.   Remember that the amend does not pertain to the other person's part in the situation.

    D.   Express your desire or ask permission to make amends. Example:

> "I am involved in a program that suggests I be aware of the harm I have done to others and that I need to take responsibility for my actions. I'd like to make amends to you. Are you OK to receive it?"

SAMPLE AMENDS
    A.   I was (scared, overwhelmed, feeling abandoned, etc.) when _____ happened between us. I ask your forgiveness for _(harm done)_ and for anything else I may have done in the past that caused you pain either by my thoughts, words, or actions. I didn't intend to cause you pain, and I ask your forgiveness.

    B.   I want to make an amend to you about _____ . For all those words that were said out of (fear, thoughtlessness, etc.) and out of my confusion, I ask your forgiveness.

1.   Select a person to whom you wish to make amends and who falls into one of the following categories.

    A.   Someone who needs to be dealt with as soon as possible.

    B.   Someone to whom you can make only partial restitution.

    C.   Someone whose situation requires that action should be deferred.

    D.   Someone with whom you will never be able to make direct personal contact.

2.   List the ways in which you would communicate the amend. _____

_____

_____

_____

_____

_____

_____

_____

AMENDS TO SELF EXERCISE

Following are some guidelines to use when making amends to yourself.

ATTITUDE
    A. Be willing to love and forgive yourself.
    B. Know what you want to say and take responsibility for your actions.
    C. Don't have unreasonable expectations of yourself.
    D. Be willing to turn it over to God.

PREPARATION
    A. Devote time to prayer and meditation. Delay the amend if you are angry or upset, and do more Step Four inventory work.
    B. Keep it simple. Explanations are not necessary.
    C. Remember the amend is to yourself and don't be concerned with the other persons involved.

SAMPLE AMENDS
    A. I was (scared, overwhelmed, feeling abandoned, etc.) when _____ happened. I forgive myself for the _(harm done)_ and anything else I may have done in the past by my thoughts, words, or actions that may have caused me harm.
    B. I want to make an amend to myself about _____ . I forgive myself for all the words that I said out of (fear, thoughtlessness, etc.) and out of my own confusion.

1.   Write an amendment letter to yourself using the above information as a guideline. _____

_____

_____

_____

_____

_____

_____

_____

_____

_____

_____

_____

_____

_____

_____

2.   What are your feelings as a result of writing this letter? _____

_____

_____

_____

_____

STEP TEN

CONTINUED TO TAKE PERSONAL INVENTORY AND, WHEN WE WERE WRONG, PROMPTLY ADMITTED IT

The initial work we have done with the Steps shows us the ineffective behavior we have been using for a considerable length of time. For many of us, the Steps may have served as an antidote to relieve some of the pain of our addictive behavior. Our commitment to continue working the Steps is an acknowledgment of our intention to improve the quality of our lives and our relationships.

1. What addictive behaviors have improved since working the Steps? _____
_____
_____
_____

2. What addictive behaviors are still lingering?_____
_____
_____
_____

Having completed Steps One through Nine, our initial housecleaning is complete, and we can begin the maintenance, sustenance, and growth phases of the Program—Steps Ten, Eleven, and Twelve. It has become apparent that spiritual growth is a lifelong process; our program must be maintained on a daily basis, one day at a time. When we accept the notion that the healing process is for the rest of our lives, the urgency to get through this work diminishes.

3. Where are you most satisfied with your progress in completing the first Nine Steps? ___
_____
_____
_____

4. Where are you most disappointed with your progress in completing the first Nine Steps?
_____
_____
_____

Some of us get the illusion that after we have completed the first Nine Steps, we are home free. We are comfortable with ourselves and no longer see a need to attend meetings regularly. We allow other activities to come into our lives, which interfere with our attending meetings, and we find excuses for missing meetings, such as being tired or having to drive too far. Some of us drop out completely. If we choose this path, we will eventually realize that our recovery is in jeopardy. We may become irritable, short-tempered, or negative in our attitudes.

5. What is your current participation in meetings? Are you attending regularly? _____

_____

_____

_____

6. What indications do you have that you are feeling comfortable and no longer need to attend meetings? _____

_____

_____

_____

At some point, we may begin to wonder if our new problems are related to the missed meetings. When we decide to return to the meetings, we will see the warmth and enthusiasm that is present. The emotional and spiritual uplift we will feel can help us get back on the path. Once we accept that we cannot afford to give up the Program, we will feel a gentle inner force compelling us to continue to develop further, to grow spiritually, one day at a time, beyond all imaginable boundaries.

7. What problems have arisen that you attribute to missing meetings? _____

_____

_____

_____

Step Ten suggests that we continue to take personal inventory and, when wrong, promptly admit it. This is an important process in our recovery; we cannot afford to hang on to useless, harmful attitudes and practices. We need to be on the lookout for signs of trying to manage our lives alone, thereby slipping into past patterns such as resentment, fear, dishonesty, or selfishness. When we see our defects crop up, it's time to ask God to remove them at once, discuss them with someone, and make amends promptly if we have caused harm.

8. What do you believe is the value of promptly admitting your wrongs? _____

_____

_____

_____

In order to successfully complete the remaining Steps of the Program, we need to acknowledge fully our need for continued spiritual development. Just as our stomachs tell us when it is time to eat, so do our souls tell us when it is time for spiritual nourishment. We recognize that we must take care of ourselves emotionally and spiritually. We begin to appreciate and love ourselves as being whole and complete. We are able to see long-range possibilities for our future successes. With the help of our Higher Power, we are able to "Let Go and Let God" so that our stress is minimized. Daily practice of Step Ten maintains our honesty and humility and allows us to continue our development.

9. What are you doing to take care of yourself spiritually? _____

_____

_____

_____

The Program suggests three types of ongoing inventories.

SPOT-CHECK INVENTORY

This is a short review of our actions, thoughts, and motives done several times a day as the need arises. Taking frequent inventories and promptly admitting our wrongs keeps us free from guilt and supports our spiritual growth.

10. Have you acquired the habit of self-appraisal? If not, how can you acquire it? _____

_____

_____

_____

During our daily activities, it is sometimes hard to recognize that seemingly nice actions are actually a signal that our old behavior is returning. An example of this is when we do a favor for someone. In the process, we think that no one else would take the time to do what we are doing. This triggers a feeling of superiority and tends to make us feel self-righteous. It can also be a sign that we are still seeking approval by "people-pleasing."

11. What are your true motives behind the nice things you do during the day? List two

examples. _____

_____

_____

_____

Another tendency is to see a wrong we are doing and blame someone else. We become angry and sometimes lose our tempers. We justify our anger rather than take responsibility for our behavior. In the end, we realize that our anger was not necessarily related to the other person's actions. It was a result of our own fears, anxieties, and feelings of insecurity.

12. Give examples of being angry at someone as a cover-up for your own inner feelings

of insecurity. _____

_____

_____

_____

DAILY INVENTORY

A daily review of the day's activities serves different and complementary purposes. It reminds us that this is a daily program, lived one day at a time. It keeps us focused on today and helps prevent us from worrying about the future or living in the past. We take this inventory much the same as in Step Four, except we are concerned only with today. The review is usually a "quickie" done on the run or just before we go to sleep.

13. How can you learn from daily inventories so that each day is better than the one before?

_____

_____

_____

As we take our daily inventory, questions arise, and we try to be as honest and humble as possible. Some of the questions we might ask ourselves are as follows:

A. Are we slipping back into control and manipulation, and are we trying to arrange the outcome of events? It is important that we recognize our behavior and ask God to correct it.

B. Are we comparing ourselves to others and feeling inferior, thus causing us to isolate ourselves? We need to reach out to our supportive friends and to acknowledge our current state, thereby renewing our self-acceptance.

C. Are we becoming obsessive/compulsive and not taking care of ourselves? Although we dislike "pressure," we may still put ourselves under all types of stress. This is a signal to slow down and proceed with moderation.

D. Are we frightened by angry people and authority figures, and do we hesitate to stand up to them? We need to remind ourselves that our ultimate authority figure, our Higher Power, is always with us.

E. Are we becoming caretakers and feeling responsible for all persons and all things? We must remember that we are responsible only for ourselves.

F. Are we depressed? If so, we need to examine the core issue that is causing us to feel sorry for ourselves.

G. Are we withholding our true feelings and finding it difficult to express our wants and needs, or are we simply giving in to others? We must overcome this so that frozen feelings do not become a pattern of behavior.

14. Which character defects show up most regularly when taking your daily inventory? _____

_____

_____

_____

15. What is your resistance to having these defects removed? _____

_____

_____

_____

LONG-TERM PERIODIC INVENTORY

This is done once or twice a year and gives us a chance to reflect on our progress from a better perspective. We can see the remarkable changes we have made, which gives us a great deal of satisfaction. We must be careful not to inflate our egos, and we must remind ourselves that our progress is a reflection of our spiritual growth. Long-term inventories help us to recognize problem areas and make the necessary corrections. We sometimes find brand new defects as a result of our new experiences.

16. What new defects have surfaced as a result of your new experiences? _____

_____

_____

_____

When a character defect reappears or a new one is identified, we can do an inventory, keeping in mind the following points:

   A. Repeating patterns are old choices of our subconscious mind and are founded upon struggle, helplessness, guilt, revenge, and disapproval.

   B. We feel safe when something is familiar, even though it is an addiction from the past.

   C. We victimize ourselves by allowing the past to possess us. We can let go of the past with the help of our Higher Power.

   D. Clinging to any character defects is a sure way to keep ourselves from obtaining what we want.

   E. Releasing an old character trait is frightening. By surrendering to our Higher Power, we can trust that we will be given one that is appropriate.

   F. Reach out. Your loving, supportive friends are an important ingredient to recovery and are available to us throughout our Program.

17. How do you include your good qualities in your personal inventory? (e.g., kindness, understanding) _____

_____

_____

_____

18. Do you realize that you are not cured of your addictive behavior but rather have been given only a daily reprieve? What is your reaction to this? _____

_____

_____

_____

It is to be expected that our inventories will show us where we are slipping into old behavior patterns. The wrong we must admit is that we violated our contract with God, which we made in the Third Step. When we turned our wills and our lives over to God's care, we agreed that we would accept God's will for us. Now we must admit that we have repossessed our wills and our lives, and we must return to Step Three. It is important to realize that pride and fear are always working to keep us from the painful task of dealing with our own faults.

19. In what areas are you slipping back into old behavior patterns? _____

_____

_____

_____

_____

20. When you have slips, why is it important to return to Step Three? _____

_____

_____

_____

Good Step Ten work has many benefits and rewards, most important of which is that it strengthens and protects our recovery. It brings rewards in several areas, such as:

A. *Personal relationships.* Troubled relationships seem to disappear. By taking inventory and admitting our wrongs promptly, the misunderstandings usually dissolve.

B. *Freedom from fear of "being found out."* Our refusal to admit wrongs is rooted in feelings of inferiority and inadequacy. We always needed to look right to other people. It is a relief to learn that we do not need to put up a false front any longer. It is okay to be ourselves.

C. *Freedom from guilt.* Guilt is one of the prices we pay for not admitting our wrongs. When we realize how harmful this is, we become more willing to face our wrongs and quickly admit them. At this point, the guilt can be removed.

D. *Ability to help others.* A surprising benefit of admitting our wrongs is that we become able to help others make similar admissions. When we admit our wrongs and stop accusing others, the way is shown to a real understanding of another's problems and to what the person can do about it.

21. In which areas of your life are you experiencing the most benefits and rewards? _____

_____

_____

_____

A final thought about Step Ten is to pay special attention to acting promptly. The sooner we admit our wrongs, the sooner the harm can be repaired to ourselves as well as to others. Delay in admitting our wrongs shows resistance to practicing Step Ten. This can be harmful because matters usually become worse. Eternal vigilance in taking a Tenth Step inventory is the price of freedom. It is our path toward freedom, and it releases us to complete the final two steps and to obtain the serenity and spirituality we are looking for.

22. How are you going to practice making a daily review of your activities so that you can promptly admit and correct your wrongs? _____

_____

_____

_____

STEP TEN DAILY INVENTORY LOG

USING THE FOLLOWING RATINGS, RECORD YOUR PERFORMANCE EACH DAY;

0=POOR   1=FAIR   2=AVERAGE   3=GOOD   4=EXCELLENT

CHARACTERISTIC (WEAKNESS)	MON.	TUE.	WED.	THUR.	FRI.	SAT.	SUN.
Anger/Resentment							
Approval seeking							
Caretaking							
Control							
Denial							
Depression/Self-pity							
Dishonesty							
Frozen feelings							
Isolation							
Jealousy							
Perfectionism							
Procrastination							
Worry (past or future)							

CHARACTERISTIC (STRENGTH)							
Forgiveness							
Generosity							
Honesty							
Humility							
Patience							
Risk-taking							
Self-nurturing							
Tolerance							
Trust							

1. What were your experiences in completing this exercise? _____
    _____
    _____

2. How did it help you to be more aware of your behavior? _____
    _____
    _____

NOTES: _____

_____

_____

_____

_____

_____

_____

_____

_____

_____

_____

_____

_____

_____

_____

_____

_____

_____

_____

_____

_____

_____

_____

_____

_____

_____

_____

_____

_____

_____

_____

_____

_____

_____

_____

_____

_____

_____

_____

_____

STEP ELEVEN

SOUGHT THROUGH PRAYER AND MEDITATION TO IMPROVE OUR CONSCIOUS CONTACT WITH GOD AS WE UNDERSTOOD HIM, PRAYING ONLY FOR KNOWLEDGE OF HIS WILL FOR US AND FOR THE POWER TO CARRY THAT OUT

Step Eleven is our opportunity to develop a deepening relationship with our Higher Power. Having developed this relationship in Steps Two and Three, we have been able to rely on it during the subsequent Steps. The relationship we developed with our Higher Power was the source of courage and strength for doing the work suggested in the Steps.

1. As a result of your diligence in working the Steps, what has been your experience in catching a glimpse of God's will? _____

   _____

   _____

   _____

At this point in working the Twelve Steps, we have no doubt noticed that to "make a decision to turn our will and our lives over to the care of God" is not a single event. It is a daily routine. Now we are being asked to "pray for knowledge of His will for us and for the power to carry that out." Turning our will over may have been more of a challenge than seeking the knowledge of God's will for us because of our persistent and repeated feelings of distrust. We were first confronted with the power of our ego (self-will) in Step One. A psychiatrist and pioneer in the field of addiction, H.M. Tiebout, M.D., wrote that the ego is made up of the persisting elements, in the adult psyche, of the original nature of the child. When infantile traits continue into adulthood, the person is referred to as being immature. The ego is the arch-enemy of our emotional sobriety.

2. How have you experienced the realization that "knowledge of God's will" comes to you only as a result of your surrendering to Him? _____

   _____

   _____

   _____

If we are periodically puzzled by the daily challenges we face from "His Majesty the Baby," we must accept that we are adult children and are still growing up. The inner child of our past tolerates frustration poorly, tends to want to do things in a hurry, and is impatient with delay. The hallmark in our adult life is the tendency to be under pressure for accomplishment. Big plans, schemes, and hopes abound. Unfortunately, these are not always matched by an ability to produce. We are clearly not doing God's will when we are expressing this behavior. "Like the cat with nine lives, the ego has a marvelous capacity to scramble back to safety—a little ruffled, perhaps, but soon operating with all its former aplomb, convinced once more that now it, the ego, can master all events and push on ahead."[4]

3. Identify behavior that you continue to demonstrate as an example of "His Majesty The Baby." _____

   _____

_____

_____

4. How does your ego get in the way of your relationship with God? _____

_____

_____

_____

Doing God's will may get so entangled with the reassertion of our old feelings and attitudes that our emotional sobriety becomes a shambles of discontent and restlessness. As we see this struggle in process, the need for our Higher Power becomes clearer.

5. What is your understanding of God's will for you at this point in your life? _____

_____

_____

_____

Step Eleven is where we focus on the daily process that is necessary for our spiritual awakening. We may have had spiritual experiences prior to this, but a spiritual experience is not a spiritual awakening. In fact, many spiritual experiences may be required before a spiritual awakening is possible. It is only through experience that the existence of a Power greater than ourselves is finally proven to us. A spiritual awakening comes when we know there is a Higher Power that has been taking care of our wills and our lives and when we know we can depend on that Higher Power to run the show from now on.

6. Identify some significant spiritual experience you have had while working the Steps.

_____

_____

_____

7. Identify situations in which you believe you have had a spiritual awakening. _____

_____

_____

_____

Step Eleven suggests that we improve our conscious contact with God as we understand Him. In order to do this, we must have already established contact. We have made conscious contact with God at least three times in the earlier Steps. In Step Three, we made a decision to turn our wills and our lives over to God's care. In Step Five, we admitted our wrongs directly to Him. In Step Seven, we humbly asked Him to remove our shortcomings. Step Eleven seeks to improve that contact, thereby enabling us to bring our Higher Power into our lives on a daily basis. It is now that we can begin to enjoy the quality relationship that is possible with Him.

8. How has your relationship with your Higher Power improved since you began working the Steps? _____

_____

_____

_____

9. In what areas do you have difficulty asking for guidance from your Higher Power? _____

_____

_____

_____

The Program implies that our Higher Power is a loving power who has only the best interests of each individual in mind. The basic premise includes the idea that this loving power wants to enrich our lives. It is exciting to realize that we can have an abundant life if we accept the protection and care of our Higher Power. The A.A. pioneers believed that this abundant life could be had for the asking. "We found that God does not make too hard terms with those who seek Him. To us, the Realm of Spirit is broad, roomy, all inclusive; never exclusive or forbidding to those who earnestly seek. It is open, we believe, to all men."[5]

10. Give examples that show your Higher Power to be a loving Power who has your best interests at heart. _____

_____

_____

_____

The means recommended to improve our conscious contact are prayer and meditation. These are the channels by which we reach Him and He reaches us. To pray is to petition God for what we would like to have Him give us, to ask for His guidance in our affairs. Prayer tells God what we want. Meditation is listening to God's will for us. Meditation techniques are designed to quiet our minds and rid us of our daily thoughts and concerns. In doing this, we allow God to enter into our minds so that we can hear His messages for us.

11. What are your past experiences of prayer when you petition God? _____

_____

_____

_____

12. What are your past experiences of meditation? _____

_____

_____

_____

Assuming we are willing, how do we pray, and what do we pray for? Many of us were taught to pray before we understood what it meant. In the beginning, we may have used the prayer "Now I lay me down to sleep, etc." We asked God to bless Mommy and Daddy and significant others. As we grew up, our dysfunctional family experiences caused some of our dreams to shatter. We may have had a tendency to blame God for not answering our prayers. Based on the principles of the Program, our attitude toward prayer changes as we work the Steps. We learn to ask for God's will for us and to accept that He knows what is best. The old habit of praying for material things diminishes, and we replace it with prayers for guidance. We begin to rely on some of the slogans and prayers, such as "Let Go and Let God" or The Serenity Prayer. Our prayers can be as simple as "God, please help me," or "Thank you, God." Any prayer is helpful if it helps the individual. The only requirement for a prayer to be successful is that it be sincere, humble, and not for our own selfish gain.

13. List examples of how you pray to God. How has your quality of prayer improved? _____

_____

_____

_____

14. In what ways do you feel uncomfortable when praying to God for help and guidance?

_____

_____

_____

Meditation is an ancient art that entails quieting the mind and not thinking. It is the channel through which we receive guidance from God. In order to meditate successfully, we must be willing to quiet our conscious mind and to remove the barriers of our conscious thoughts. This is difficult for some of us because we are unaccustomed to sitting still and relaxing. Meditation helps to calm us emotionally and to relax us physically. It helps us release energy we normally expend in keeping our emotions in high gear and our bodies taut.

15. Because you have opened your mind to inspiration, in what ways have you discovered

that meditation can reveal solutions you had not dreamed of? _____

_____

_____

_____

An overview of prayer and meditation in a given day may be outlined as follows:

I. **BEGINNING OF THE DAY:**
    A. Review our plans for the day.
        1. Ask God to direct our thoughts and actions.
            a. To keep us free from self-pity, dishonesty, selfishness.
            b. To give us the guidance needed to take care of any problems.
        2. Ask God for freedom from self-will.
            a. To prevent our making requests unless others will be helped.
            b. To stop us from praying for our own selfish ends.

II. DURING THE DAY, IN MOMENTS OF INDECISION OR FEAR:

A. Ask God for inspiration and guidance.

B. Ask God for clear, intuitive answers.

C. Reflect on Step Three and turn it over.
   1. Relax and breathe deeply several times.
   2. Be aware of any desire to struggle with a situation or person.

D. Pray to God as often as necessary during the day.
   1. "God, please remove this _____." (feeling, obsession, addiction, etc.)
   2. "Thy will be done."

E. If possible, call a support person simply to acknowledge what is happening.

III. END OF THE DAY:

A. Review the events of the day by practicing Step Ten and taking a personal inventory.

B. Take time to pray for knowledge of His will for us.

C. Acknowledge that this review is not intended to cause obsessive thinking, worry, remorse, or morbid reflection.

D. Pray to God, asking:
   1. For forgiveness.
   2. For guidance in corrective action we need to take.

The methods of prayer and meditation may vary; however, it is our intentions and the prayer content that matter. Our commitment is primarily to deepen our relationship and open our communication with God. This means being honest, sharing our innermost selves, confessing our wrong doings, and bringing our failings to Him for forgiveness. By our dedication to prayer and meditation, and by becoming aware of God's unconditional love and forgiveness, we are empowered to continue our life in awareness of His constant presence. If we continue to pray with patience and trust, the result can be only humility, love, and faith.

16. In what ways has Step Eleven changed your view of the method or use of prayer and meditation? _____

_____

_____

_____

The importance of Step Eleven is that it tells us precisely the things to pray for. In this Step of spiritual awakening, we pray only for knowledge of His will for us and for the power to carry that out. The word "only" emphasizes the fact that from now on, we pray for nothing else except His will and the courage to go forward and do what He makes us want to do.

17. What resistance do you experience when you read the part of Step Eleven which states to pray "only" for knowledge of His will and for the power to carry that out? _____

_____

_____

_____

The miracle of this Step is that it changes our past method of praying into a form of meditation, whether we know how to meditate or not. Praying only for His will and for the power to carry that out drives all our personal concerns from our consciousness and allows us to concentrate only on His concerns. This very prayer empties our mind of our own wants and allows God to enter.

18. What thoughts have you had that you assumed were from God, only to discover that they were unconscious desires (e.g., praying for a new relationship leads us into past behavior)?

_____

_____

_____

19. What was the result of acting on these illusions? _____

_____

_____

_____

If we have thoroughly placed our will in His care and pray, we must trust that our will is being directed by Him. The power to carry that out will be the courage to do so, and He will also give us that.

Seeking guidance is a tricky matter because we are so accustomed to running our lives rigidly and making demands on God. Our own desires and opinions are so much a part of us that we are likely to view the will of a Higher Power in terms of our own feelings.

20. How is your own ego and self-will getting in the way of your praying for God's will?

_____

_____

_____

In Step Eleven, we concede complete willingness to accept God's will and whatever terms are offered. We are no longer in a position to demand anything, and the best we can hope for is relief from our agony. We stop making demands on our Higher Power and let things work out in a natural way.

21. Give examples that show you are not putting demands on your Higher Power and are willing to let things work out in a natural way. _____

_____

_____

_____

Prayer and meditation are used to improve our conscious contact with God as we understand Him. If we are progressing satisfactorily with Step Eleven, there will be signs along the way. One sign is a deep sense of gratitude, accompanied by a feeling of belonging in the world at last. Another is our feeling of being worthy. We have a sense of being guided and sustained as we proceed with our activities.

22. What is your opinion of your self-worth today? _____
_____
_____
_____

23. In what areas of your life do you have a sense of gratitude? _____
_____
_____
_____

It is not always easy to maintain this new way of life. We may face boredom and disillusionment after the early stages of inspiration and excitement. Step Eleven reminds us of the need to maintain the wonderful way of life we've been given. It is no quick fix. It is really Steps Two and Three practiced on a daily basis. It can be our guide for the rest of our lives. If we understand and follow it carefully, some of the changes in our lives will border on the miraculous. We can have continuous recovery along with the qualities we were seeking but never found.

24. How is boredom a problem for you now that you are achieving some peace and serenity in your life? _____
_____
_____
_____

Step Eleven does exact a price, and we must pay it if we expect favorable results. There is a price in giving up the self-will that led us into trouble. Part of the price is facing the need to become open-minded and being willing to change. Doing God's will can be as simple as accepting that there is no strain in doing God's Will. As soon as we accept it as our own, we will experience complete peace and joy. Unless we experience this, we are refusing to acknowledge His will for us. And finally, Step Eleven calls for faith and persistence—the very qualities that we applied so wrongly to our compulsive behavior.

25. How willing are you to allow change, now, compared to your willingness prior to working the Steps? _____
_____
_____
_____

26. What is your current level of faith and persistence? _____
_____
_____
_____

4. Harry M. Tiebout, *The Ego Factors In Surrender in Alcoholism*, (New York: Journal of Studies on Alcohol, Inc.)
5. *Alcoholics Anonymous*. Third Edition, A.A. World Services, Inc (New York, NY), p.46.

JUST FOR TODAY

I will take a good look at myself and see that I have many addictive and compulsive traits that have become dominant in my life. I am at the mercy of these traits and unable to manage them. Seeing this, I admit that I need help.

I will acknowledge the presence of a Power greater than myself who has created me, is aware of all my needs, and is fully capable of healing me and restoring me to a condition of clarity and stability. This power is God as I choose to understand Him.

I will let go of the inclination to figure out my problems with my mind. No more analyzing . . . no more questioning. I now make a conscious decision to turn my life and my will over to the care and keeping of God. I surrender the thinking that tells me I must "run my own show" and make my own life happen. I am ready to be a TRANSFORMED (changed) person, beginning right now.

I will release the past, letting go of any guilt or regrets about what happened "back then." Finding fault or blaming myself and/or others keeps me stuck in the past.

I will forgive myself and others for the way we've been. I realize that our actions have risen out of fear and insecurity. I now allow myself and others to "be." I no longer pass judgment on our lives, our chosen paths, or our pattern of growth.

I will drop all anxiety about the future. I will live THIS DAY with as much joy, trust, and serenity as I can, realizing that this day is all I can handle.

I will let go of my tendencies to be dependent on persons, possessions, and patterns to fulfill me. I recognize that these things are only a temporary part of my existence and cannot provide the lasting security, inner peace, or true freedom that I yearn to experience on a daily basis.

I will take responsibility for all aspects of my life: my choices, my feelings, my physical and mental health, my spiritual well-being, my paths of growth, and the principles and values by which I live.

I will utilize all the energies within me that contribute to the betterment of my life and to the lives of others (e.g., expressing honesty, integrity, and kindness). To all else, I firmly say, "No, thank you."

I will thank God for the opportunity to be set free from old attitudes and behavior patterns that prevent me from moving in the direction of my needed healing.

I will willingly share with others the wisdom, peace, and strength I have received through this Program.

I will go forth into this day with enthusiasm, believing in my own value and worthiness, and with the determination to enjoy this day and give it my positive best, come what may.

JUST FOR TODAY EXERCISE

Review your expectations for today. Remember to ask for knowledge of God's will for you, and for the power to carry that out.

1. Just for today, I will _____

    _____

    _____

    _____

    _____

2. Just for today, I will _____

    _____

    _____

    _____

    _____

3. Just for today, I will _____

    _____

    _____

    _____

    _____

4. Just for today, I will _____

    _____

    _____

    _____

    _____

5. Just for today, I will _____

    _____

    _____

    _____

    _____

6. Just for today, I will _____

    _____

    _____

    _____

    _____

NOTES: _____

_____

_____

_____

_____

_____

_____

_____

_____

_____

_____

_____

_____

_____

_____

_____

_____

_____

_____

_____

_____

_____

_____

_____

_____

_____

_____

_____

_____

_____

_____

_____

_____

_____

_____

_____

_____

_____

_____

STEP TWELVE

HAVING HAD A SPIRITUAL AWAKENING AS A RESULT OF THESE STEPS, WE TRIED TO CARRY THIS MESSAGE TO OTHERS AND TO PRACTICE THESE PRINCIPLES IN ALL OUR AFFAIRS.

The Twelfth Step is where we were headed when we started our journey toward recovery and a spiritual awakening. As we worked our way through the Steps, something inside told us that there was hope at the end of the journey. The mystery surrounding the Twelve Steps is that they really work for those who are willing to surrender to a Higher Power. A.A. tells us: "The joy of living is the theme of the Twelfth Step, and action is its key word."[6] If we have practiced the other eleven steps to the best of our ability, we will have a spiritual awakening.

1. List three ways in which the Twelve Steps have helped you to experience the joy of living. _____

_____

_____

_____

The process of working the Steps can be likened to the transformation of a caterpillar to a butterfly. The caterpillar is not clear that it is going to be a butterfly. Everything that is part of its death and re-birth in the cocoon must be experienced. The story is told of a man who noticed a cocoon on a bush in his yard. As he started to pull it from the bush and throw it away, he noticed the end was opening and a butterfly was struggling to escape. In an effort to help the emerging butterfly, he took it inside and carefully cut the cocoon away with a razor blade. The butterfly feebly crawled from the open cocoon and, within a few hours, died. It needed the strength it would have gained from the struggle to free itself in order to survive in the outside world. In a like manner, our working the Steps is something that only we can do. Any attempts to have another person do our work or find answers for us inhibits our own recovery and limits our ability to become strong.

2. Explain your understanding of the butterfly story as it applies to your needs to have your own experiences. _____

_____

_____

_____

Our spiritual awakening is a gift that places us in a new state of consciousness and being. It is usually accompanied by a complete change in values. Where there used to be darkness, we now begin to see light. For most of us, the awakening is subtle and can only be viewed with hindsight. The maturity we gain by working the Steps enables us to view many experiences, often painful, as being spiritual in nature. Our awakening can be viewed as the sum total of these individual experiences. With each of them, we can identify in some way or another how our Higher Power is guiding us.

3. Which spiritual awakenings have been the most rewarding for you? _____

_____

_____

_____

4. How can you further enhance your spiritual awakenings? _____

_____

_____

_____

We become able to do, feel, and believe things that are not possible by our own resources. We find in ourselves a degree of honesty, humility, peace of mind, and love that we had not previously possessed. Our new values are based on a realistic view of ourselves as children of God, and we recognize a need for emotional and spiritual balance in our lives. With the help of our Higher Power, we have discovered new abilities in ourselves we never knew existed.

5. In what ways do you see yourself as a child of God, needing emotional and spiritual

balance? _____

_____

_____

_____

It is important to remember that our spiritual awakening is an ongoing process. It may have begun early in the Steps, but it continues for the rest of our lives. It is not a distinct event with a clear beginning and ending. As our spiritual awakening continues, we become more lovable, make friends more easily, and feel more comfortable with people. Our relationships with our families improve as we draw closer, yet we recognize each other's independent identity. We no longer have unrealistic expectations of ourselves, and we accept ourselves for who we are.

6. Evaluate your current relationships with your family and friends. _____

_____

_____

_____

7. How do these compare to your previous relationships? _____

_____

_____

_____

Because we know this Program works and is working for us, we are ready to carry the message to others. This is the means by which the Program grows, prospers, and flourishes. We have healthy tools for reaching out to those people who are in bondage, as we once were. The message we carry is a liberating one. Sharing the message strengthens our own recovery and continues our spiritual growth. The gift we receive in return may be new strength or new insights. It is also a means of helping ourselves continue to grow emotionally. Whatever it may be, we can be assured of satisfaction from our desire to help another human being. The most effective way of convincing people of the value of the Steps is to be ourselves the way God created us. This alone will reflect examples of our miraculously transformed lives.

8. Given that you have something to share with others, are you willing to carry this message to those in need? _____

_____

_____

_____

9. In what specific way are you planning to accomplish this? (e.g., service work) _____

_____

_____

_____

There is no formal qualification for working this Step, other than the willingness and the desire to tell our stories as honestly as we can. This is one time when being ourselves is the gift we give to others. This can happen anywhere when we are called upon to do volunteer work, share in meetings, or interact with co-workers and family members. As we share our story with others and help them to recognize their need, we are learning to be humble and to express ourselves honestly. When we carry the message, we share how the Twelve Steps have transformed our lives, taking time to share our miraculous experiences with others who are in need of help. We tell them what we used to be like, what happened to us as a result of the Steps, and what we are like now. As we share our experience, strength, and hope with newcomers, we help them find a way to solve their own problems, look at themselves honestly, and stop finding fault with others.

10. Given your expanded self awareness from working the Steps, how are you now clear that you will never have enough insight into another's life to tell him what is best to do? _____

_____

_____

_____

Working with newcomers can be a rewarding experience. These people are usually troubled, confused, and resentful. They are looking for "instant relief." They need guidance, and we can help them to understand that the Program represents pain and hard work. The rewards and miracles far outweigh the pain. We need to encourage the newcomers to be gentle with themselves and to take the Program one day at a time. This is also a growth experience for us as we reflect back on where we were when someone introduced us to the Program. When carrying the message, we must emphasize that the decision to join the Program is an individual one that is made by most of us when we have suffered enough, are tired of hurting, or in other words, when we have "hit bottom."

11. Are you clear that sharing with others can do more for you than it can for them? Explain how carrying the message is an obligation you have to yourself. _____

_____

_____

_____

A recurring message throughout the Twelve Steps is the importance of humility and obedience to our Higher Power. As we diligently practice these principles in our daily affairs, the key factor for success is our relationship with our Higher Power. Working closely with our Higher Power helps us stay on the right course by our considering Him as a source of guidance and support. We realize now that we cannot achieve peace in the world until we have achieved peace within ourselves. We cannot achieve peace and serenity within ourselves independently of a Higher Power. We must individually admit we are powerless and begin to work on our spiritual development, one day at a time, for the rest of our lives.

12. Examine the degree to which you rely on your Higher Power. Give examples. _____

_____

_____

_____

We can view our progress by comparing where we were with where we are now. Are we less isolated and no longer afraid of authority figures? Have we stopped seeking approval and become accepting of ourselves as we really are? Are we more selective of the people we choose to form relationships with, and are we able to keep our own identity while in a relationship? Have we developed the ability to express our feelings? Have our fears lessened? Have a lot of our character defects been transformed into assets, and are we behaving in a sane manner? If we are able to answer affirmatively to the above, we have come a long way since Step One when our character defects were active and damaging.

13. Describe the progress you see in yourself as a result of completing this Twelve Step Workbook. _____

_____

_____

_____

As we practice this new behavior in our daily affairs, life in general seems to start working better. For some of us, our examples in family and work environments have a positive effect on those around us, and we can see recovery in our loved ones. This is truly a measure of our progress and of our determination to change our lives and our behavior. The more committed we are to living the Steps on a daily basis, the more likely we are to have a continual spiritual awakening for the remainder of our lives.

14. What changes do you see in your family and friends that you can attribute to changes in your own behavior? _____

_____

_____

A key factor in practicing the Steps in all our affairs is to become accustomed to "living" the Steps. If we are truly committed to working the Steps, we will see that most of our problems can be resolved through the Steps. The practice of taking a problem through all the Steps is very healing and can be done in a relatively short time. In doing this, we find support and guidance from our Higher Power. The end result usually provides an inner peace and an ability to deal directly with the problem.

15. Having completed this workbook, what are you planning to do in order to continue "living" the Steps, one day at a time? _____

_____

_____

_____

We have no doubt found that the program really does work in all areas of our lives. All we need to do is be willing to try and to let go. We find that as our faith in our Higher Power increases, we become more willing to trust. As our trust grows, we become willing to turn over our lives more readily, and this furthers our spiritual development. The process is gradual, regenerative, and never-ending. We slowly become God-oriented and thus learn the meaning of love, growth, and serenity.

16. Have you set up a network of support for yourself? If so, how can you use this network to remind you that, in carrying the message, actions speak louder than words? _____

_____

_____

_____

KEEP COMING BACK. IT WORKS.

6. *Twelve Steps and Twelve Traditions*, Alcoholics Anonymous World Services, Inc., (New York), p. 109.

TWELVE STEP EXERCISE

1. Identify a situation or condition in your life that is currently a source of resentment, fear, sadness, or anger. It may involve relationships (family, work, or sexual), work environment, health, or self-esteem. Write a concise statement describing the situation and indicating your concern. _____

   _____

   _____

2. Use the following exercise to apply the principles of the Twelve Steps to the above.

   STEP ONE: In what ways are you powerless, and how is this situation showing you the unmanageability of your life? _____

   _____

   _____

   _____

   STEP TWO: How do you see your Higher Power as helping you to restore your sanity?

   _____

   _____

   _____

   STEP THREE: How does being willing to turn your life over to the care of God assist you in dealing with this?_____

   _____

   _____

   _____

   STEP FOUR: What character defects have surfaced? (e.g., fear of abandonment or authority figures, control, approval seeking, obsessive/compulsive behavior, rescuing, excessive responsibility, unexpressed feelings) _____

   _____

   _____

   _____

   STEP FIVE: Admit your wrongs, at least to God and yourself._____

   _____

   _____

   _____

STEP SIX: Are you entirely ready to have God remove the character defects that have surfaced? _____

_____

_____

_____

STEP SEVEN: Can you humbly submit to God and ask Him to remove your shortcomings? If not, what is your resistance? _____

_____

_____

_____

STEP EIGHT: Make a list of the persons being harmed. _____

_____

_____

_____

STEP NINE: What amends are necessary, and how will you make the amends? _____

_____

_____

_____

STEP TEN: Review the above Steps to be sure that nothing has been overlooked. _____

_____

_____

_____

STEP ELEVEN: Take a moment for prayer or meditation, asking God for knowledge of His will for you. _____

_____

_____

_____

STEP TWELVE: How can your understanding and spiritual awakening assist you in dealing with your problem?

_____

_____

_____

_____

_____

NOTES: _____

_____

_____

_____

_____

_____

_____

_____

_____

_____

_____

_____

_____

_____

_____

_____

_____

_____

_____

_____

_____

_____

_____

_____

_____

_____

_____

_____

_____

_____

_____

_____

_____

_____

_____

_____

_____

APPENDIX ONE

METHODS OF STUDY

There are two methods of effectively using this workbook: self-study and group study. The information in this appendix is intended as a guideline to assist you in successfully completing the workbook. The information contained in the self-study section also applies to group study.

SELF-STUDY

Read the entire Step narrative for each Step before reading the questions. Then return to the beginning of the narrative and answer the questions. This will give you a better perspective of the material.

As you proceed through the Steps, it is important to pace yourself. Work on only one Step at a time and allow sufficient time to complete each process. This may take a week or longer. Allow yourself time to digest the material and reflect on its meaning. Be patient with yourself. This is an opportunity to see how impatience can interfere with your effectiveness. Don't be discouraged if Steps One, Two, and Three seem overwhelming to you. It is in these three Steps that we form the foundation for working the Program.

Depending upon the level of your commitment to do the writing, you may discover that you will want to go through the Twelve Steps more than one time. The Twelve Step Program is a lifelong process to be used daily as a part of our lives. It is not expected or intended that this workbook be your only involvement with working the Twelve Steps.

Wherever possible, share your insights with someone you trust. Communicating your discoveries to another human being can work miracles. In many Anonymous programs, this person is referred to as a sponsor. A sponsor is familiar with the Steps, and his insights and experiences can be invaluable. It is important to be aware that your listener is not there to give advice. The healing is a result of your relationship with your Higher Power.

If this workbook is your first exposure to the Twelve Steps and you are not presently attending an Anonymous Twelve Step Program meeting, it is suggested that you find a meeting to attend. The following listings will help you to identify which program is best for you. Other resources can be found in the library or in the telephone directory under "social service organizations" or "crisis intervention".

GROUP STUDY

Once you have identified a group you feel comfortable with, you are ready to start a committed Step Study Writing Workshop. The following information will assist you in forming the workshop. Appendix Two includes guidelines to be used by the meeting secretary. The focus of this information is on using this workbook. There is additional information available on "Adult Children" or "Co-Dependents" which can be included in the workshop. A suggested reading list is contained in Appendix Four.

Starting a Step Study is not difficult. It involves making an announcement at one or more Anonymous meetings. It is possible that many people will show up only one or two times to check out the meeting. It is suggested that the meeting be closed to newcomers on the third week. The workshop is designed to last twenty-three weeks, in accordance with the Appendix Three weekly writing exercises. Appendix Two includes a sample announcement format.

Even though you start the workshop and function as secretary, it is important to have a different leader each week. It is recommended that leadership rotate by "family group" rather than by individuals. This gives each "family group" an opportunity to lead on a periodic basis. The meeting formats included in Appendix Two have proven to be effective. They are intended as suggestions only. The main idea is to keep the format simple so that the workshop participants can focus mainly on working the Steps.

Previous workshops have revealed that trust develops most quickly when there are small "family groups" with a maximum of seven individuals. For example, if there are twenty-four participants, it is recommended that the workshop be formed into four "family groups", each containing six members. The small "family groups" will be together to complete the evening's writing exercise and to share within their group for a specified period of time. The final portion of the meeting is devoted to sharing in one all-inclusive group. There is no ideal arrangement, other than to keep the working "family groups" small.

When people get together to work on material as challenging as the Steps, it is important that everyone be in agreement regarding the commitment to work the Steps as a group. The participation agreements in Appendix Two, which are read and signed by each individual, help to support this commitment.

During the workshop, various issues among the participants will surface. There will possibly be dissension within the small groups as to compatibility. In previous workshops, these issues were resolved without making changes within the group. It was found that the struggles within each family group were re-enactments of family of origin situations. Leaving the groups as originally established for the duration of the workshop fosters growth and strengthens the bonds within the family group.

As participants surrender to the guidance of their Higher Power, many problems will be dealt with in a more constructive manner. As Adult Children we are inclined to be caretakers, enablers and people pleasers. This manifest itself by our inability to be confrontive toward inappropriate, incongruent, or self-destructive behavior. Instead we tend to be overly nice to each other. In keeping with the intention of having a safe environment for the "family group" members to alter old patterns of behavior, heavy confrontation is not needed. Straightforward feedback is important, with communication being expressed as one's personal experience of a given situation.

Due to our early exposure to negative behavior (e.g., resentment, greed, sexual abuse, dishonesty, gluttony, envy, laziness) and negative feelings (e.g., self-pity, sadness, insecurity, worry, fear of rejection, fear of abondonment) they seem normal to us. As we progress through the Steps, this negativity will be reduced. We will experience growth in all areas by increasing our self-worth and self-esteem. Therefore, positive feelings and positive thought need to be frequently encouraged. It is helpful to take time periodically during the workshop to ask people's feelings about the progress of the workshop. This enables the facilitator to encourage open and honest communication within the entire group.

There is no right way to work the material. Each person has something to contribute in whatever way he or she chooses to work the material. The results will be varied, but each participant will experience some degree of growth and change.

If this is your first experience in a committed Step Study Writing Workshop, you are encouraged to be in touch with individuals who are familiar with this material. Please feel free to contact us at (619) 275-1350 or write the Publisher if you have any questions relative to the Step Study.

SELF HELP RESOURCES

Adult Children of Alcoholics
Central Service Board
PO Box 35623
Los Angeles, CA 90035
(213) 464-4423

Al-Anon/Alateen Family Group
Headquarters, Inc.
Madison Square Station
New York, New York 10010
(212) 683-1771

Alcoholics Anonymous World Services, Inc.
468 Park Avenue South
New York, New York 10016
(212) 686-1100

Debtors Anonymous
P.O. Box 20322
New York, N.Y. 10025-9992

Emotions Anonymous
P.O. Box 4245
St. Paul, MN. 55104

Gamblers Anonymous
P.O. Box 17173
Los Angeles, CA 90017

Narcotics Anonymous
World Service Office
16155 Wyandotte Street
Van Nuys, CA 91406
(818) 780-3951

National Association for Children of
Alcoholics
31706 Coast Highway, Suite 201
South Laguna, CA 92677
(714) 499-3889

National Clearinghouse for Alcohol
Information
P.O. Box 1908
Rockville, Maryland 20850
(301) 468-2600

National Council on Alcoholism
12 West 21st Street
New York, New York 10010
(212) 206-6770

Overeaters Anonymous
World Service Office
2190 190th Street
Torrance, CA 90504
(213) 320-7941

Are you Ready for the Next Step in Recovery?

A writing Step Study is starting using
The 12 Steps ... A Way Out

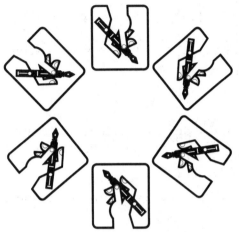

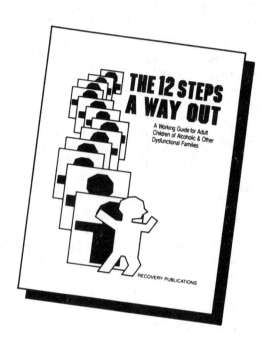

Beginning Date: _____

Day: _____

Time: _____

Location: _____

Writing Step Study Overview

Following is an outline of what to expect from participating in a Writing Step Study. Although the writing focuses on the book, **The 12 Steps — A Way Out**, it is important to include other reading material while you are working the Steps.

1. During the first three weeks, the meeting remains open so that anyone interested in finding out about the meeting format is welcomed to do so.

2. After the third week, small family groups are formed. These groups are an important part of the Step Study process, and help to develop trusting, supportive relationships during the weeks that follow.

3. Beginning with the fourth week, the meeting is facilitated by each family group on a rotating basis. The meeting format is in Appendix Two of the workbook.

4. Two weeks are spent on most of the steps.

5. It is recommended that you read the workbook material, and complete as much of the writing as possible.

6. The weekly writing exercise, located in Appendix Three, is the central focus of the weekly meeting. Time is spent at the beginning of the meeting to complete the exercise, and is used as the basis for the family sharing.

7. It is important to keep in mind that you are doing this work for your own personal growth. Set your own pace and accept your progress without putting unrealistic expectations on yourself.

8. This program is worked **one day at a time.**

SAMPLE STEP STUDY WRITING WORKSHOP PARTICIPATION AGREEMENT

I, _____, agree to participate with my family in working the TWELVE STEPS and also agree to:

1. Give my maximum effort. To try sincerely by actively participating in weekly meetings and by being in contact with my Step Study family between meetings.

2. Be as positively idealistic as possible. I will expect results, healing, recovery, and miracles.

3. Support my family by giving my undivided attention to others when they are sharing and by not interrupting, fixing, or taking another person's inventory.

4. Be as honest as possible.

5. Humbly submit to the method and do my best to suspend negative judgment. (Humble means teachable. We don't have the power or knowledge to do this alone. Submit means to surrender. Regardless of how we feel, we will do the work anyway.)

6. Schedule time between weekly meetings to work on the step, especially the written work to be brought to, and shared at, the meeting.

7. Study the step thoroughly by reading from a variety of sources.

8. Keep my commitment to myself and to my family by attending the weekly meetings and by doing my utmost to schedule everything else around the meeting.

9. Share my experience, strength, and hope during the step study meeting. (I am no longer a victim.)

10. Be willing and able to accept a higher level of discomfort, thus accepting the ongoing process of recovery.

11. Refrain from intellectualizing when sharing (stay out of my head) and to do the best I can to identify and share my feelings, for example, joy, sadness, elation, depression, anger, love, hate, guilt, acceptance, hurt, loneliness, support, inadequacy, or power.

12. Incorporate the "Five Qualities of Recovery" into my daily life:
    A. Attend meetings.
    B. Work the steps.
    C. Pray and meditate daily.
    D. Use the telephone.
    E. Begin and end each day with the first three steps.

SAMPLE SECRETARY WORKSHEET
STEP STUDY WRITING WORKSHOP PARTICIPATION AGREEMENT

SECRETARY:

When reading the participation agreements, it is helpful to use the secretary's worksheet in order to emphasize the importance of the participation agreements.

1. Give my maximum effort. To try sincerely by actively participating in weekly meetings and by being in contact with my Step Study family between meetings.

    A. Step One is the 100% step.
        1) The first three steps build inner strength and a reliance on our Higher Power.
        2) Violation of Step One in our lives is what gets us into trouble.

2. Be as positively idealistic as possible. I will expect results, healing, recovery, and miracles.

    A. The intention is to develop skills and relationships which will enhance your:
        1) Ability to be self-parenting.
        2) Ability to be self-nurturing.
        3) Ability to create a network of support.

    B. Acknowledge our humanity by working Step One to the utmost of our ability:
        1) Work the steps consistently.
        2) Expect results.
        3) Expect healing.
        4) Expect recovery.
        5) Expect miracles.

3. Support my family by giving my undivided attention to others when they are sharing and by not interrupting, fixing, or taking another person's inventory.

    A. We will support each other in nurturing, ministering, and healing.
        1) When someone is sharing, give the person your undivided attention.
        2) Don't interrupt.
        3) Be as honest as possible.
        4) Be genuinely there. We give support through example.
        5) Our Higher Power works through us to enable us to experience breaking through barriers.
        6) Suspend judgment or evaluation of progress.
        7) Stop co-dependent behavior, which means supporting others in their problems.

4. Be as honest as possible.

5. Humbly submit to the method and do my best to suspend negative judgment.
    (Humble means teachable. We don't have the power or knowledge to do this alone.)
    (Submit means to surrender. Regardless of how we feel, we will do the work anyway.)

    A. The format is different from a general meeting. Structure and writing are part of the process. The procedures used in this group are directly related to the purpose intended.

    B. The major differences from other meetings are:
        1) There is a commitment to write; it is not group consciousness to question the writing. Follow the directions whether you agree with them or not.

2) If your primary need is emotional support, this is not the proper group. There are other more suitable groups, or you can start your own.

6. Schedule time between weekly meetings to work on the step, especially the written work to be brought to, and shared at, the meeting.

   A. Meeting before the regular workshop time may allow for family group interaction that the workshop does not provide. You and your family group will have to assess the need for this as you get to know each other.

7. Study the step thoroughly by reading from a variety of sources.

8. Keep my commitment to myself and to my family by attending the weekly meetings and by doing my utmost to schedule everything else around the meeting.

   A. Attendance; commitment to self and group.
      1) Schedule other activities around meetings.
      2) An emergency is a bona-fide excuse not to attend.
      3) Harmony and results in this Step Study will depend largely on how the family group interacts.

9. Share my experience, strength, and hope during the step study meeting. (I am no longer a victim.)

   A. Non-support is demonstrated by:
      1) Giving advice.
      2) Taking responsibility for others and trying to fix them.
      3) Being dishonest.
      4) Taking inventories. It does not work to point out what's wrong with another person's inventory.

   B. What people need, they get, either in the meeting or in their daily life; it's not necessary that you provide what they need.

10. Be willing and able to accept a higher level of discomfort, thus accepting the ongoing process of recovery.

    A. Be willing to accept discomfort.
       1) An indication of lack of recovery is "No pain, no gain."
       2) Follow through. Be willing to do something that doesn't feel good.

11. Refrain from intellectualizing when sharing (stay out of my head) and to do the best I can to identify and share my feelings, for example, joy, sadness, elation, depression, anger, love, hate, guilt, acceptance, hurt, loneliness, support, inadequacy, or power.

12. Incorporate the "Five Qualities of Recovery" into my daily life:

    A. Attend meetings.
    B. Work the steps.
    C. Pray and meditate daily.
    D. Use the telephone.
    E. Begin and end each day with the first three steps.

SAMPLE MEETING GUIDELINES FOR SECRETARY

This guideline is to be used by the secretary or the person who is leading the meeting for the evening.

1. Before the regular meeting begins, read through the evening's writing exercise.

2. Ask each group to phone anyone who is absent in order to support their next attendance.

3. Remind the groups to keep the individual sharing focused on the Step being worked. Encourage recovery-type sharing.

    a. Sharing is to be focused on *individual* experience, strength, and hope in working the Steps.

    b. It is not necessary for everyone to share.

    c. Allow equal time for everyone in the group to share.

4. Encourage each group to meet at another time for more opportunities to process writing and to deepen "family group" bonding and trust. An alternative to meeting is to use the telephone regularly.

5. Encourage group members to share outside reading. Emphasize the importance of doing outside reading to broaden one's understanding of the Steps.

6. Be as loving, supportive, and positive as possible, recognizing you won't always feel this way.

7. Be a good friend who is willing to listen yet not give advice.

SAMPLE STEP STUDY WRITING WORKSHOP FORMAT
INTRODUCTORY MEETING

REWARD PROMPTNESS BY STARTING THE MEETING ON TIME

7:45 P.M. (Allow approximately 25 minutes for the following information)
BEGIN MUSIC. (Background music useful during writing, if available.)

PASS OUT *THE GOALS, THE PROMISES, THE TWELVE STEPS.*

STOP MUSIC.

"Good evening! Welcome to the _____ Step Study Writing Workshop. My name is _____, and I am an Adult Child. As such, I was exposed to the influence of alcoholism during my childhood by an adult (parent, grandparent, etc.). As a result, my own behavior has been affected. Surprisingly, you may have the characteristics of an Adult Child without having biological parents who are, themselves, alcoholics."

"Please join me in the Serenity Prayer."

"I have asked _____ to read *The Goals.*"
"I have asked _____ to read *The Promises.*"
"I have asked _____ to read *The 12 Steps.*"

"Our Seventh Tradition states that we are self-supporting through our own contributions. We ask for your contribution at this time to avoid interrupting the meeting."

AFTER THE SEVENTH TRADITION:

"Welcome to each of you. This Step Study Workshop is not easy. If you have been attending meetings and reading books and literature for at least six months, you have begun to confront the denial that has kept you in your dysfunctional behavior. You will find writing on each of the Twelve Steps a powerful healing tool. Working the Steps can be overwhelming in the beginning stages of your recovery. Unless you have been in the Program approximately six months, you are asked to seriously consider not joining this Step Study. Instead, we suggest you attend open meetings, open Step Study meetings, and read several books relating to Adult Children of Alcoholics and Co-Dependency. This will make you better prepared for the writing workshop. One of the first lessons in recovery is to know your boundaries and participate only in those activities that support your recovery."

"During the first two weeks, you will have an opportunity to experience the ongoing format of this workshop. You will be asked to make a decision by the third meeting. The process requires twenty-three weeks of work, play, and growth."

"You will find new relationships emerging as you spend time with the group and share their experience, strength, and hope. The quality of these relationships may be unlike any other you have experienced."

"The principal purpose of this meeting is to facilitate healing and recovery. You will be asked to do some unnatural things: like trusting others, practicing healthy dependence and interdependence, learning to listen, and sharing your feelings. You will have the opportunity to experience what a healthy family can be like."

8:10 P.M. (Allow approximately 30 minutes for the following material)
(HAVE COPIES OF THE WRITING STEP STUDY OVERVIEW TO HAND OUT)

"Please refer to page #128 to read the Writing Step Study Overview.

"Following is an outline of what to expect from participating in a Writing Step Study. Although the writing focuses on the book, *THE 12 STEPS — A WAY OUT*, it is important to include other reading material while you are working the Steps.

1. During the first three weeks, the meeting remains open so that everyone interested in finding out about the meeting format is welcomed to do so.

2. After the third week, small family groups are formed. These groups are an important part of the Step Study process, and help to develop trusting, supportive relationships during the weeks that follow.

3. Beginning with the fourth week, the meeting is facilitated by each family group on a rotating basis. The meeting format is in Appendix Two of the workbook.

4. Two weeks are spent on most of the Steps.

5. It is recommended that you read the workbook material, and complete as much of the writing as possible.

6. The weekly writing exercise, located in Appendix Three, is the central focus of the weekly meeting. Time is spent at the beginning of the meeting to complete the exercise, and is used as the basis for the family sharing.

7. It is important to keep in mind that you are doing this work for your own personal growth. Set your own pace and accept your progress without putting unrealistic expectations on yourself.

8. This program is worked one day at a time.

"As the facilitator of this meeting I want you all to understand that I will lead only the first four meetings. By the fifth meeting 'family groups' will have been formed and each group will have the responsibility of leading the meeting.

"This is an introductory meeting and is intended to provide an overview of the Step Study Writing Workshop using the workbook *THE 12 STEPS — A WAY OUT*.

(HAVE A COPY OF PAGE #1 FROM STEP ONE AVAILABLE TO BE HANDED OUT)

"For those of you who have not purchased a copy of the workbook, I have available a sample Step One page which I will hand out now. For those who have the workbook please turn to page #1 so we can review the format of the writing to be done between the weekly meetings. It is important to note that before attempting to write responses to the questions relative to each Step, reading the entire step narrative will provide an overview of the material on which you are to write. Before each weekly meeting, reading the Step narrative and responding to the questions will significantly improve the value received from participating in the Step Study.

"The Steps are a process wherein you begin to see the possibility of correcting behavior which is damaging to yourself and others. Your willingness to commit to this workshop will help you face making changes in your behavior. It is important not to obsess on the writing. Do the best you can, and work at your own pace. There are no right or wrong answers, and no right or wrong ways to complete the exercises.

"As the facilitator, my purpose is to be your trusted servant. I will be working the Steps with you. Please understand that I am here, as I believe you are, to share my experience, strength and hope.

"The principal quality required to successfully complete this workbook is to be willing to engage in the process one day at a time, one meeting at a time. Bring the body and the mind will follow. Learn to trust that a Higher Power will take care of the outcome.

"We will spend the next 20 minutes openly discussing the weekly writing from the workbook."

8:40 P.M. (Allow approximately 40 minutes for the following material)
END OF FIRST DISCUSSION SEGMENT

(HAVE A COPY OF STEP #1 - WEEK #1 WRITING EXERCISE. PAGE 147 TO BE HANDED OUT)

"For those who do not have the workbook I am going to hand out a sample of Step #1 - Week #1 writing exercises.

"Approximately fifteen minutes is allocated to the writing exercise at each Step Study meeting. This is followed by approximately forty minutes of 'Family Group' sharing. The sharing is either about the evening's writing exercise or the workbook writing on the Step.

"Following the 'Family Group' sharing, the meeting is opened to include all 'Family Groups', and approximately twenty five minutes is spent on general sharing.

"The meeting lasts from 7:45 P.M. to 9:30 P.M. (Approximately 1¾ hours)

"At this time the meeting is open for further discussion on questions relative to the workshop."

9:20 P.M. (Allow approximately 10 minutes to conclude meeting)
END OF GROUP SHARING

"The material that will be used from the workbook each week is principally to guide you through the writing processes dealing with each Step. It is not intended to provide all the information on each Step. It will be helpful to read the books that are listed as references."

ASK FOR ANY ANNOUNCEMENTS

"Reminder! What you hear at this meeting, leave at this meeting! It is not for public disclosure or gossip. Please respect the privacy of what was shared here tonight."

"Will everyone please clean up after themselves and help re-arrange the room?

"Will all who care to, join me in the closing prayer?"

9:30 P.M.
ADJOURN

SAMPLE STEP STUDY WRITING WORKSHOP FORMAT
WEEK #1

REWARD PROMPTNESS BY STARTING THE MEETING ON TIME

7:45 P.M. (Allow approximately 15 minutes for the following material)
BEGIN MUSIC. (Background music useful during writing, if available.)

PASS OUT *THE GOALS, THE PROMISES, THE TWELVE STEPS.*

STOP MUSIC.

"Good evening! Welcome to the _____ Step Study Writing Workshop. My name is _____, and I am an Adult Child. As such, I was exposed to the influence of alcoholism during my childhood by an adult (parent, grandparent, etc.). As a result, my own behavior has been affected. Surprisingly, you may have the characteristics of an Adult Child without having biological parents who are, themselves, alcoholics."

"Please join me in the Serenity Prayer."

"I have asked _____ to read *The Goals.*"
"I have asked _____ to read *The Promises.*"
"I have asked _____ to read *The 12 Steps.*"

"Our Seventh Tradition states that we are self-supporting through our own contributions. We ask for your contribution at this time to avoid interrupting the meeting."

AFTER THE SEVENTH TRADITION:

"Welcome to each of you. This Step Study Workshop is not easy. If you have been attending meetings and reading books and literature for at least six months, you have begun to confront the denial that has kept you in your dysfunctional behavior. You will find writing on each of the Twelve Steps a powerful healing tool. Working the Steps can be overwhelming in the beginning stages of your recovery. Unless you have been in the Program approximately six months, you are asked to seriously consider not joining this Step Study. Instead, we suggest you attend open meetings, open Step Study meetings, and read several books relating to Adult Children of Alcoholics and Co-Dependency. This will make you better prepared for the writing workshop. One of the first lessons in recovery is to know your boundaries and participate only in those activities that support your recovery."

"During the first two weeks, you will have an opportunity to experience the ongoing format of this workshop. You will be asked to make a decision by the third meeting. The process requires twenty-three weeks of work, play, and growth."

"You will find new relationships emerging as you spend time with the group and share their experience, strength, and hope. The quality of these relationships may be unlike any other you have experienced."

"The principal purpose of this meeting is to facilitate healing and recovery. You will be asked to do some unnatural things: like trusting others, practicing healthy dependence and interdependence, learning to listen, and sharing your feelings. You will have the opportunity to experience what a healthy family can be like."

"If you decide to join this writing workshop, you will be asked to make several commitments, some of which are as follows:

A. Make a sincere effort to do the work. Some of the material will cause discomfort.
 1. Attend regularly. Bring the body; the mind will follow.
 2. Participate and share to the best of your ability.
 3. Allow for change. It takes courage, strength, and patience. You don't have to do it all alone or all at once.
B. Participate in healthy family-type interaction.
 1. Tell the truth and keep your word.
 2. Be willing to accept support, as well as give it.
 3. Identify and accept your limits: physically, mentally, and emotionally.
C. Accept the fact that this is a spiritual program coming from love.
 1. Healing is done by a spiritual Power greater than ourselves.
 2. The leaders are but trusted servants.
D. Engage in recovery-type sharing as distinguished from dumping.
 1. Recovery-type sharing is clearly expressing how one's program is working to heal old patterns of addictive, compulsive or obsessive behavior.
 2. Dumping is stating your problems and looking at yourself as a victim, rather than someone working a program of recovery.

8:00 P.M. (Allow approximately 10 minutes for the following material)

(HAVE COPIES OF THE WRITING STEP STUDY OVERVIEW TO HAND OUT)
(REFER TO EITHER PAGE #128 OR THE INTRODUCTORY WEEK AND READ IT)

8:10 P.M. (Allow approximately 20 minutes for the following material)
 A. ASK THAT SMALL GROUPS OF 4-7 BE FORMED, DEPENDING ON THE TOTAL GROUP SIZE.
 B. REFER TO WEEK #1 WRITING EXERCISE.
 C. HAVE A COPY OF PAGE #1 FROM STEP ONE AND WEEK #1 WRITING EXERCISE FOR THOSE WHO DO NOT HAVE THE WORKBOOK.

PRIOR TO START OF WRITING EXERCISE:

"There will be fifteen minutes allowed to complete the individual writing process. I will give you a two-minute warning to allow you to complete your work."

8:30 P.M. (Allow approximately 30 minutes for the following material)
END OF WRITING TIME:

"Sharing your written work within each group will last thirty minutes. I'll give you a three-minute warning to complete the sharing."

"Do not intellectualize when sharing. Stay out of your head. Share the feelings you experienced while writing to the best of your ability. (e.g., joy, sadness, anger, love, guilt, hurt, loneliness, support)

9:00 P.M. (Allow approximately 25 minutes for the following material)
END OF SMALL GROUP SHARING:

"Please re-arrange your chairs into one large circle. The meeting is now open to sharing your experiences of tonight."

9:25 P.M. (Allow 5 minutes to conclude meeting)
FIVE MINUTES BEFORE END OF THE MEETING:

"The material that will be used from the workbook each week is principally to guide you through the writing processes dealing with each Step. It is not intended to provide all the information on each Step. It will be helpful to read the books that are listed as references."

ASK FOR SECRETARY ANNOUNCEMENTS.

"Newcomers are invited to remain after the meeting to discuss any questions they have relative to the Step Study."

"Reminder! What you hear at this meeting, leave at this meeting! It is not for public disclosure or gossip. Please respect the privacy of what was shared here tonight."

"Will everyone please clean up after themselves and help re-arrange the room?"

"Will all who care to, join me in a closing prayer?"

9:30 P.M.
ADJOURN

MEETING PREPARATION WEEK #1

1.   HAVE COPIES OF PAGE #1 STEP ONE NARRATIVE FOR THOSE WHO DO NOT HAVE A WORKBOOK.

2.   HAVE COPIES OF THE WRITING STEP STUDY OVERVIEW FOR THOSE WHO DO NOT HAVE A WORKBOOK.

3.   HAVE COPIES OF WEEK #1 WRITING EXERCISE FOR THOSE WHO DO NOT HAVE A WORKBOOK.

SAMPLE STEP STUDY WRITING WORKSHOP FORMAT
WEEK #2

REWARD PROMPTNESS BY STARTING THE MEETING ON TIME

7:45 P.M. (Allow approximately 15 minutes for the following material)
BEGIN MUSIC. (Background music useful during writing, if available.)

PASS OUT *THE GOALS, THE PROMISES, THE TWELVE STEPS* .

STOP MUSIC.

"Good evening! Welcome to the _____ Step Study Writing Workshop. My name is _____, and I am an Adult Child. As such, I was exposed to the influence of alcoholism during my childhood by an adult (parent, grandparent, etc.). As a result, my own behavior has been affected. Surprisingly, you may have the characteristics of an Adult Child without having biological parents who are, themselves, alcoholics."

"Please join me in the Serenity Prayer."

"I have asked _____ to read *The Goals.*"
"I have asked _____ to read *The Promises.*"
"I have asked _____ to read *The 12 Steps.*"

"Our Seventh Tradition states that we are self-supporting through our own contributions. We ask for your contribution at this time to avoid interrupting the meeting."

AFTER THE SEVENTH TRADITION:

"Welcome to each of you. This Step Study Workshop is not easy. If you have been attending meetings and reading books and literature for at least six months, you have begun to confront the denial that has kept you in your dysfunctional behavior. You will find writing on each of the Twelve Steps a powerful healing tool. Working the Steps can be overwhelming in the beginning stages of your recovery. Unless you have been in the Program approximately six months, you are asked to seriously consider not joining this Step Study. Instead, we suggest you attend open meetings, open Step Study meetings, and read several books relating to Adult Children of Alcoholics and Co-Dependency. This will make you better prepared for the writing workshop. One of the first lessons in recovery is to know your boundaries and participate only in those activities that support your recovery."

"You will find new relationships emerging as you spend time with the group and share their experience, strength, and hope. The quality of these relationships may be unlike any other you have experienced."

"The principal purpose of this meeting is to facilitate healing and recovery. You will be asked to do some unnatural things: like trusting others, practicing healthy dependence and interdependence, learning to listen, and sharing your feelings. You will have the opportunity to experience what a healthy family can be like."

"If you decide to join this writing workshop, you will be asked to make several commitments, some of which are as follows:

   A. Make a sincere effort to do the work. Some of the material will cause discomfort.

1. Attend regularly. Bring the body; the mind will follow.
2. Participate and share to the best of your ability.
3. Allow for change. It takes courage, strength, and patience. You don't have to do it all alone or all at once.

B. Participate in healthy family-type interaction.
1. Tell the truth and keep your word.
2. Be willing to accept support, as well as give it.
3. Identify and accept your limits: physically, mentally, and emotionally.

C. Accept the fact that this is a spiritual program coming from love.
1. Healing is done by a spiritual Power greater than ourselves.
2. The leaders are but trusted servants.

D. Engage in recovery-type sharing as distinguished from "dumping".
1. Recovery-type sharing is clearly expressing how one's program is working to heal old patterns of addictive compulsive or obsessive behavior.
2. "Dumping" is stating your problems and looking at yourself as a victim, rather than someone working a program of recovery.

8:00 P.M. (Allow approximately 20 minutes for the following material)
"In a few minutes, I am going to pass out *Participation Agreements*, which are the ground rules that enable everyone to join in this Step Study Writing Workshop. The *Participation Agreements* establish the guidelines you are asked to use during this workshop. The effectiveness and success of the individuals who preceded you is the basis for these agreements. Your willingness to accept them is your choice. The level of your success will hinge on your desire to be supportive and to abide by the agreements. Keep the agreements and bring them with you next week." Families are selected at random by dividing the name cards equally into groups. No consideration is given to "special" arrangements. This may sound controlling, but has been proven to be a safe and "non-judgmental" approach to family selection. It is a big step toward "letting go".

A. ASK FOR SMALL GROUPS OF 4-7 TO BE FORMED, DEPENDING ON THE TOTAL GROUP SIZE.
B. REFER TO PARTICIPATION AGREEMENT (PAGE #129).
C. READ THE AGREEMENTS, USING THE FACILITATOR'S COPY FOR ELABORATION.
D. REFER TO WEEK #2 WRITING EXERCISE.
E. HAVE A COPY OF THE PARTICIPATION AGREEMENT AND WEEK #2 WRITING EXERCISE FOR THOSE WHO DO NOT HAVE THE WORKBOOK.
F. PASS OUT 3X5 NOT CARDS AND ASK EACH INDIVIDUAL TO COMPLETE THE CARD LISTING THEIR FIRST NAME, LAST INITIAL AND TELEPHONE NUMBER. (THESE CARDS WILL BE USED TO FORM FAMILY GROUPS PRIOR TO THE NEXT MEETING)

8:20 P.M. (Allow 10 minutes for writing)
PRIOR TO START OF WRITING EXERCISE:
"There will be ten minutes allowed to complete the individual writing process. I will give you a two-minute warning to allow you to complete your work."

8:30 P.M. (Allow 30 minutes for family group sharing)
END OF WRITING TIME:

"Sharing your written work within each group will last thirty minutes. I'll give you a three-minute warning to complete the sharing."

"Do not intellectualize when sharing. Stay out of your head. Share the feelings you experienced while writing to the best of your ability. (e.g., joy, sadness, anger, love, guilt, hurt, loneliness, support).

9:00 P.M. (Allow 25 minutes for large group sharings)
END OF SMALL GROUP SHARING:

"Please re-arrange your chairs into one large circle. The meeting is now open to sharing your experiences of tonight."

9:25 P.M. (Allow 5 minutes to conclude meetings.)
FIVE MINUTES BEFORE END OF THE MEETING:

"The material which will be used from the workbook each week is principally to guide you through the writing processes dealing with each Step. It is not intended to provide all the information on each Step. It will be helpful to read the books that are listed as references."

ASK FOR SECRETARY ANNOUNCEMENTS.

"Reminder! What you hear at this meeting, leave at this meeting! It is not for public disclosure or gossip. Please respect the privacy of what was shared here tonight."

"Will everyone please clean up after themselves and help re-arrange the room?"

"Will all who care to, join me in a closing prayer?"

9:30 P.M.
ADJOURN

MEETING PREPARATION WEEK #2

1.   HAVE COPIES OF PAGE #1 STEP ONE NARRATIVE FOR THOSE WHO DO NOT HAVE A WORKBOOK.

2.   HAVE COPIES OF THE WRITING STEP STUDY OVERVIEW FOR THOSE WHO DO NOT HAVE A WORKBOOK.

3.   HAVE COPIES OF WEEK #2 EXERCISE FOR THOSE WHO DO NOT HAVE A WORKBOOK.

4.   HAVE COPIES OF THE PARTICIPATION AGREEMENT FOR THOSE WHO DO NOT HAVE A WORKBOOK.

5.   HAVE 3X5 CARDS AVAILABLE TO BE COMPLETED BY PARTICIPANTS.

SAMPLE STEP STUDY WRITING WORKSHOP FORMAT
WEEK #3 - #23

REWARD PROMPTNESS BY STARTING THE MEETING ON TIME

7:45 P.M. (Allow 15 minutes to begin meeting)
BEGIN MUSIC. (Background music useful during writing, if available)

PASS OUT *THE GOALS, THE PROMISES, THE TWELVE STEPS*.

"Will everyone please be seated with their respective family groups."

STOP MUSIC.

"Good evening! Welcome to the _____ Step Study Writing Workshop. My name is _____, and I am your trusted servant for tonight."

"Please join with me in the Serenity Prayer."

"I have asked _____ to read *The Goals*."
"I have asked _____ to read *The Promises* or *The Participation Agreement*."
"I have asked _____ to read *The Twelve Steps*."

"Our Seventh Tradition states that we are self-supporting through our own contributions. We ask for your contribution at this time to avoid interrupting the meeting. Will each family please pass the envelope?"

8:00 P.M. (Allow 15 minutes for writing)
"The time for writing will be fifteen minutes, and the time for family sharing will be forty minutes, after which we will all join together."

START MUSIC.

"Sharing can be from your Step writing this past week or from the Step work done tonight. The writing and sharing topic for tonight is on Step #____."

8:15 P.M. (Allow 40 minutes for family group sharing)
GIVE A THREE-MINUTE WARNING PRIOR TO THE END OF FAMILY WRITING TIME.

8:55 P.M. (Allow 5 minutes for forming large group)
GIVE A THREE-MINUTE WARNING PRIOR TO THE END OF FAMILY SHARING TIME.

9:00 P.M. (Allow 30 minutes for large group sharing)
STOP MUSIC. ANNOUNCE THAT IT IS TIME TO FORM THE OPEN GROUP.

"Please open the groups so as to include everyone. The time available for sharing is twenty-five minutes. Does someone desire to share about the Step work that took place within their family tonight or this past week?"

9:25 P.M. (Allow 5 minutes to conclude meeting)
ASK FOR SECRETARY ANNOUNCEMENTS.

"The Family Group leading the meeting next week is _____."

"Reminder! What you hear at this meeting, leave at this meeting! It is not for public disclosure or gossip. Please respect the privacy of what was shared here tonight."

"Will everyone please clean up after themselves and help re-arrange the room?"

"Will all who care to, join me in a closing prayer?"

9:30 P.M.
ADJOURN

MEETING PREPARATION WEEK #3

1. HAVE FAMILY GROUPS ASSIGNED. THIS IS DONE BY SORTING THE 3X5 CARDS RANDOMLY INTO FAMILY GROUPS.

2. PREPARE A MASTER LIST OF ALL PARTICIPANTS DIVIDED INTO FAMILY GROUPS. THE LIST IS TO INCLUDE:
   FIRST NAME, LAST INITIAL AND TELEPHONE NUMBER

MEETING PREPARATION WEEK #4 - #23

NO ADDITIONAL PREPARATION NEEDED AS FACILITATOR.

THE GOALS
THE OPPOSITE OF "THE PROBLEM"

1. I feel comfortable and involved with people and authority figures.

2. I have a strong identity and give myself approval.

3. I accept and use personal criticism in a positive way.

4. I am becoming free from trying to fulfill my sick abandonment need.

5. As I face my own victim role, I am attracted by strengths and understand weaknesses in my love and friendship relationships.

6. I am getting well through loving and focusing on myself.

7. It feels great to stand up for myself.

8. I enjoy peaceful serenity.

9. I love people who love and take care of themselves.

10. I am free to feel and express my feelings even when painful.

11. I have a healthy sense of self-esteem.

12. I am freed from the fear of abandonment in relationships as I rely more and more on my Higher Power.

13. Through the ACA group, I examine and release para-alcoholic behaviors I learned while living with the family disease of alcoholism.

14. I am an actor in this world.

THE PROMISES

1. We are going to know a new freedom and a new happiness.

2. We will not regret the past nor wish to shut the door on it.

3. We will comprehend the word serenity, and we will know peace.

4. No matter how far down the scale we have gone, we will see how our experience can benefit others.

5. That feeling of uselessness and self-pity will disappear.

6. We will lose interest in selfish things and gain interest in our fellows.

7. Self-seeking will slip away.

8. Our whole attitude and outlook will change.

9. Fear of people and economic insecurity will leave us.

10. We will know intuitively how to handle situations that used to baffle us.

11. We will suddenly realize that God is doing for us what we could not do for ourselves.

THE TWELVE STEPS

1. We admitted we were powerless over the effects of alcoholism . . . that our lives had become unmanageable.

2. Came to believe a power greater than ourselves could restore us to sanity.

3. Made a decision to turn our will and our lives over to the care of God as we understood Him.

4. Made a searching and fearless moral inventory of ourselves.

5. Admitted to God, to ourselves, and to another human being the exact nature of our wrongs.

6. Were entirely ready to have God remove all these defects of character.

7. Humbly asked Him to remove our shortcomings.

8. Made a list of all persons we had harmed and became willing to make amends to them all.

9. Made direct amends to such people whenever possible except when to do so would injure them or others.

10. Continued to take personal inventory and, when we were wrong, promptly admitted it.

11. Sought through prayer and meditation to improve our conscious contact with God *as we understood Him*, praying only for knowledge of His will for us and for the power to carry that out.

12. Having had a spiritual awakening as a result of these Steps, we tried to carry this message to others and to practice these principles in all our affairs.

APPENDIX THREE

STEP ONE
PROCESSES AND QUESTIONS FOR WEEK #1 (Step #1 - Week #1)

We admitted we were powerless over the effects of alcoholism-
that our lives had become unmanageable.

1. What is your main objective in choosing to participate in this workshop? (See questions 18-21, Step One narrative.) _____

_____

_____

_____

_____

_____

_____

_____

_____

_____

_____

_____

_____

2. What anxieties do you have regarding the idea of a weekly commitment for a six-month period? _____

_____

_____

_____

_____

_____

_____

_____

_____

_____

_____

_____

_____

ALLOCATE EQUAL TIME FOR EACH FAMILY MEMBER. PLEASE LIMIT INDIVIDUAL SHARING TO WHAT WAS WRITTEN. ALLOW TIME FOR FEEDBACK FROM FAMILY MEMBERS AFTER WRITING HAS BEEN SHARED.

STEP ONE
PROCESSES AND QUESTIONS FOR WEEK #2 (Step #1 - Week #2)

We admitted we were powerless over the effects of alcoholism-
that our lives had become unmanageable.

1. List specific events that happened *last week* that are an example of your powerlessness.

    _____
    _____
    _____
    _____
    _____
    _____
    _____
    _____
    _____
    _____
    _____
    _____
    _____
    _____
    _____

2. List specific events that happened *last week* that are an example that your life is unmanageable. _____

    _____
    _____
    _____
    _____
    _____
    _____
    _____
    _____
    _____
    _____
    _____
    _____
    _____

ALLOCATE EQUAL TIME FOR EACH FAMILY MEMBER. PLEASE LIMIT INDIVIDUAL SHARING TO WHAT WAS WRITTEN. ALLOW TIME FOR FEEDBACK FROM FAMILY MEMBERS AFTER WRITING HAS BEEN SHARED.

STEP TWO
PROCESSES AND QUESTIONS FOR WEEK #3 (Step #2 - Week #1)

Came to believe that a Power greater than ourselves could restore us to sanity.

1.   Where are you in relation to your acceptance of a Higher Power? _____
_____
_____
_____
_____
_____
_____
_____
_____

2.   List specific events that happened *last week* that demonstrate irrational (insane) behavior?
_____
_____
_____
_____
_____
_____
_____
_____

3.   As part of tonight's family group sharing, introduce yourself and share a brief story about your background. Also, restate for your family group your main objective in choosing to participate in this workshop. (See Week #1 writing exercise.) _____
_____
_____
_____
_____
_____
_____
_____
_____

ALLOCATE EQUAL TIME FOR EACH FAMILY MEMBER. PLEASE LIMIT INDIVIDUAL SHARING TO WHAT WAS WRITTEN. ALLOW TIME FOR FEEDBACK FROM FAMILY MEMBERS AFTER WRITING HAS BEEN SHARED.

STEP TWO
PROCESSES AND QUESTIONS FOR WEEK #4 (Step #2 - Week #2)

Came to believe that a Power greater than ourselves could restore us to sanity.

1. What is your response to the statement: "It isn't necessary (or possible) to *understand* God. We need only to accept that the Power is there and to know it can restore us to sanity." _____

    _____

    _____

    _____

    _____

    _____

    _____

    _____

2. What difficulties are you having in accepting a Higher Power? Identify any childhood memories that may be getting in your way. _____

    _____

    _____

    _____

    _____

    _____

    _____

    _____

    _____

3. What action have you taken to allow your Higher Power to come alive in your life and thereby experience His presence? _____

    _____

    _____

    _____

    _____

    _____

    _____

    _____

ALLOCATE EQUAL TIME FOR EACH FAMILY MEMBER. PLEASE LIMIT INDIVIDUAL SHARING TO WHAT WAS WRITTEN. ALLOW TIME FOR FEEDBACK FROM FAMILY MEMBERS AFTER WRITING HAS BEEN SHARED.

STEP THREE
PROCESSES AND QUESTIONS FOR WEEK #5 (Step #3 - Week #1)

Made a decision to turn our will and our lives over
to the care of God as we understood Him.

_____

1. Summarize briefly your response to the following questions contained in the Step Three narrative. (See questions 19-22.)

    "MADE A DECISION"_____
    _____
    _____
    _____

    "TO TURN OUR WILL AND OUR LIVES OVER"_____
    _____
    _____
    _____

    "TO THE CARE OF GOD" _____
    _____
    _____
    _____

    "AS WE UNDERSTOOD HIM" _____
    _____
    _____
    _____

2. What are the main areas in your life that need to be turned over to God? Explain. _____
    _____
    _____
    _____
    _____
    _____
    _____
    _____
    _____
    _____
    _____

ALLOCATE EQUAL TIME FOR EACH FAMILY MEMBER. PLEASE LIMIT INDIVIDUAL SHARING TO WHAT WAS WRITTEN. ALLOW TIME FOR FEEDBACK FROM FAMILY MEMBERS AFTER WRITING HAS BEEN SHARED.

STEP THREE
PROCESS AND QUESTIONS FOR WEEK #6 (Step #3 - Week #2)

Made a decision to turn our will and our lives over
to the care of God as we understood Him.

1. The purpose of the *HIGHER POWER EXERCISE* was to identify key role models in your life. How did the writing process assist you in discovering qualities you are attracted to in others? How did it help you in accepting a Higher Power? _____

_____

_____

_____

_____

_____

_____

_____

_____

_____

_____

_____

2. List specific situations that occurred last week in which you successfully worked Step Three. How did you feel when you turned it over? _____

_____

_____

_____

_____

_____

_____

_____

_____

_____

_____

_____

_____

ALLOCATE EQUAL TIME FOR EACH FAMILY MEMBER. PLEASE LIMIT INDIVIDUAL SHARING TO WHAT WAS WRITTEN. ALLOW TIME FOR FEEDBACK FROM FAMILY MEMBERS AFTER WRITING HAS BEEN SHARED.

STEP FOUR
PROCESSES AND QUESTIONS FOR WEEK #7 (Step #4 - Week #1)

Made a searching and fearless moral inventory of ourselves.

1. Identify the areas in your life in which denial is most active. _____
    _____
    _____
    _____
    _____
    _____
    _____
    _____
    _____
    _____
    _____
    _____
    _____

2. What kind of support do you want from your family group to help you complete
    Step Four? (e.g., telephone support, meeting outside of regular meetings) Please ask
    for what you want. People can't read your mind. _____
    _____
    _____
    _____
    _____
    _____
    _____
    _____
    _____
    _____
    _____
    _____
    _____
    _____

ALLOCATE EQUAL TIME FOR EACH FAMILY MEMBER. PLEASE LIMIT
INDIVIDUAL SHARING TO WHAT WAS WRITTEN. ALLOW TIME FOR FEEDBACK
FROM FAMILY MEMBERS AFTER WRITING HAS BEEN SHARED.

STEP FOUR
PROCESSES AND QUESTIONS FOR WEEK #8 (Step #4 - Week #2)

Made a searching and fearless moral inventory of ourselves

1. Briefly describe your progress in preparing for your Step Four inventory. List any difficulties. _____

    _____

    _____

    _____

    _____

    _____

    _____

    _____

    _____

    _____

    _____

    _____

    _____

    _____

2. Refer to the *RESENTMENT AND FEAR EXERCISES*. Discuss in greater length your main resentment and your main fear. _____

    _____

    _____

    _____

    _____

    _____

    _____

    _____

    _____

    _____

    _____

    _____

    _____

ALLOCATE EQUAL TIME FOR EACH FAMILY MEMBER. PLEASE LIMIT INDIVIDUAL SHARING TO WHAT WAS WRITTEN. ALLOW TIME FOR FEEDBACK FROM FAMILY MEMBERS AFTER WRITING HAS BEEN SHARED.

STEP FOUR
PROCESSES AND QUESTIONS FOR WEEK #9 (Step #4 - Week #3)

Made a searching and fearless moral inventory of ourselves.

1. How did the *CHARACTER TRAIT EXERCISE* help you in identifying your behavior as it relates to your character strengths and weaknesses? _____

_____

_____

_____

_____

_____

_____

_____

_____

2. Which of your "weaknesses" do you most frequently have difficulty with? _____

_____

_____

_____

_____

_____

_____

_____

_____

_____

3. Which of your "strengths" are you having the most success with? _____

_____

_____

_____

_____

_____

_____

_____

_____

ALLOCATE EQUAL TIME FOR EACH FAMILY MEMBER. PLEASE LIMIT INDIVIDUAL SHARING TO WHAT WAS WRITTEN. ALLOW TIME FOR FEEDBACK FROM FAMILY MEMBERS AFTER WRITING HAS BEEN SHARED.

STEP FIVE
PROCESSES AND QUESTIONS FOR WEEK #10 (Step #5 - Week #1)

Admitted to God, to ourselves, and to another human being the exact nature of our wrongs.

1. Write briefly how you currently feel toward your Step family group. _____
    _____
    _____
    _____
    _____
    _____

2. Up to now, what have you been unwilling to ask for from your family group? _____
    _____
    _____
    _____
    _____
    _____

3. What are you willing to ask for now? _____
    _____
    _____
    _____
    _____
    _____

4. What have you been unwilling to give to your family group?_____
    _____
    _____
    _____
    _____
    _____

5. What are you willing to give or commit to your family group? _____
    _____
    _____
    _____
    _____
    _____

ALLOCATE EQUAL TIME FOR EACH FAMILY MEMBER. PLEASE LIMIT
INDIVIDUAL SHARING TO WHAT WAS WRITTEN. ALLOW TIME FOR FEEDBACK
FROM FAMILY MEMBERS AFTER WRITING HAS BEEN SHARED.

STEP FIVE
PROCESSES AND QUESTIONS FOR WEEK #11 (Step #5 - Week #2)

Admitted to God, to ourselves, and to another human being the exact nature of our wrongs.

1. Summarize what you learned and/or experienced from working the Fifth Step. _____
_____
_____
_____
_____
_____
_____
_____
_____
_____
_____
_____
_____
_____
_____

2. Describe your personal experiences during your Fifth Step sharing with another person. Were you able to follow the suggested format? _____
_____
_____
_____
_____
_____
_____
_____
_____
_____
_____
_____
_____
_____

ALLOCATE EQUAL TIME FOR EACH FAMILY MEMBER. PLEASE LIMIT INDIVIDUAL SHARING TO WHAT WAS WRITTEN. ALLOW TIME FOR FEEDBACK FROM FAMILY MEMBERS AFTER WRITING HAS BEEN SHARED.

STEP SIX
PROCESSES AND QUESTIONS FOR WEEK #12 (Step #6 - Week #1)

Were entirely ready to have God remove all these defects of character.

"BROKEN DREAMS"

As children bring their broken toys
    with tears for us to mend,
I brought my broken dreams to God
    because He was my friend.
But then, instead of leaving Him
    in peace to work alone,
I hung around and tried to help
    with ways that were my own.
At last, I snatched them back and cried,
    "How can you be so slow?"

    "My child," he said,
    "What could I do?"
    "You never did let go."

Author unknown

1. How does the "Broken Dreams Prayer" bring you in touch with your willingness to "let go?" _____

_____

_____

_____

_____

_____

_____

2. Identify behavior changes that you attribute to your "being entirely ready" to have God remove your character defects. _____

_____

_____

_____

_____

_____

_____

ALLOCATE EQUAL TIME FOR EACH FAMILY MEMBER. PLEASE LIMIT INDIVIDUAL SHARING TO WHAT WAS WRITTEN. ALLOW TIME FOR FEEDBACK FROM FAMILY MEMBERS AFTER WRITING HAS BEEN SHARED.

STEP SEVEN
PROCESSES AND QUESTIONS FOR WEEK #13 (Step #7 - Week #1)

Humbly asked Him to remove our shortcomings.

"PARADOXES OF PRAYER"

I asked God for strength, that I might achieve
    I was made weak, that I might learn humbly to obey . . .
I asked for health, that I might do greater things
    I was given infirmity, that I might to better things . . .
I asked for riches, that I might be happy
    I was given poverty, that I might be wise . . .
I asked for power, that I might have the praise of men
    I was given weakness, that I might feel the need of God . . .
I asked for all things, that I might enjoy life
    I was given life, that I might enjoy all things . . .
I got nothing that I asked for—but everything I had hoped for
    Almost despite myself, my unspoken prayers were answered
I am among all, most richly blessed!

(c) Universal Press Syndicate

1. How does the above prayer assist you in achieving the humility needed for Step Seven?

    _____
    _____
    _____
    _____
    _____
    _____
    _____

2. List experiences that show how your relationship with your Higher Power is improving.

    _____
    _____
    _____
    _____
    _____
    _____
    _____

ALLOCATE EQUAL TIME FOR EACH FAMILY MEMBER. PLEASE LIMIT INDIVIDUAL SHARING TO WHAT WAS WRITTEN. ALLOW TIME FOR FEEDBACK FROM FAMILY MEMBERS AFTER WRITING HAS BEEN SHARED.

STEP EIGHT
PROCESSES AND QUESTIONS FOR WEEK #14 (Step #8 - Week #1)

Made a list of all persons we had harmed,
and became willing to make amends to them all.

1. Examine your present participation in telephone contact with your Step Study family members. During the coming week, will you be willing to make arrangements to contact your family members? Share with your family how you *feel* about this request. _____

_____
_____
_____
_____
_____
_____

2. Describe the person to whom you have caused the most harm. What are your experiences with that person that warrant amends? _____

_____
_____
_____
_____
_____
_____

3. Which of your character defects contributed to this situation? _____

_____
_____
_____
_____
_____
_____
_____

ALLOCATE EQUAL TIME FOR EACH FAMILY MEMBER. PLEASE LIMIT INDIVIDUAL SHARING TO WHAT WAS WRITTEN. ALLOW TIME FOR FEEDBACK FROM FAMILY MEMBERS AFTER WRITING HAS BEEN SHARED.

STEP EIGHT
PROCESSES AND QUESTIONS FOR WEEK #15 (Step #8 - Week #2)

Made a list of all persons we had harmed,
and became willing to make amends to them all.

The following are three of the fifteen *Traits of a Healthy Family*, as described by Dolores Curran in her book under the same title.

COMMUNICATION
Trait #1: The "healthy" family communicates and listens.

AFFIRMING AND SUPPORTING
Trait #2: The "healthy" family affirms and supports one another.

GETTING HELP
Trait #15: The "healthy" family admits to, and seeks help with, problems.

1. What efforts did you make to contact your Step Study family last week as part of being supported in making your amends list? _____

   _____

   _____

   _____

2. If you did have contact, was your experience one of support and encouragement, particularly as described in Trait #2? _____

   _____

   _____

   _____

3. What difficulties are you having in making your amends list? _____

   _____

   _____

   _____

4. Share with your Step Study family how you perceive the openness of communication within your family group. Also share your progress with Step Eight. _____

   _____

   _____

   _____

ALLOCATE EQUAL TIME FOR EACH FAMILY MEMBER. PLEASE LIMIT INDIVIDUAL SHARING TO WHAT WAS WRITTEN. ALLOW TIME FOR FEEDBACK FROM FAMILY MEMBERS AFTER WRITING HAS BEEN SHARED.

STEP NINE
PROCESSES AND QUESTIONS FOR WEEK #16 (Step #9 - Week #1)

Made direct amends to such people wherever possible,
except when to do so would injure them or others.

1. Select a person with whom you can make only partial restitution. List the ways in which you would communicate the amend. (See AMENDS TO OTHERS EXERCISE, Page 97.) _____

    _____

    _____

    _____

    _____

    _____

    _____

2. Ask one of your family members to hear the amend. (Separate into pairs.) _____

    _____

    _____

    _____

    _____

    _____

    _____

    _____

3. After completing the above, share with your family members your experience of making and receiving the amend. _____

    _____

    _____

    _____

    _____

    _____

    _____

    _____

ALLOCATE EQUAL TIME FOR EACH FAMILY MEMBER. PLEASE LIMIT INDIVIDUAL SHARING TO WHAT WAS WRITTEN. ALLOW TIME FOR FEEDBACK FROM FAMILY MEMBERS AFTER WRITING HAS BEEN SHARED.

STEP NINE
PROCESSES AND QUESTIONS FOR WEEK #17 (Step #9 - Week #2)

Made direct amends to such people wherever possible,
except when to do so would injure them or others.

1. List some highlights of the amends letter to yourself. (See AMENDS TO SELF EXERCISE.) _____

_____

_____

_____

_____

_____

_____

_____

2. Ask one of your family members to hear the amend. (Separate into pairs.)_____

_____

_____

_____

_____

_____

_____

_____

_____

_____

3. After completing the above, share with your family members the experience of making and receiving the amend._____

_____

_____

_____

_____

_____

_____

ALLOCATE EQUAL TIME FOR EACH FAMILY MEMBER. PLEASE LIMIT INDIVIDUAL SHARING TO WHAT WAS WRITTEN. ALLOW TIME FOR FEEDBACK FROM FAMILY MEMBERS AFTER WRITING HAS BEEN SHARED.

STEP TEN
PROCESSES AND QUESTIONS FOR WEEK #18 (Step #10 - Week #1)

Continued to take personal inventory and, when we were wrong, promptly admitted it.

1. Review your actions last week, as recorded on your DAILY INVENTORY LOG. In what area did you perform best? In what area did you perform poorly? _____

_____

_____

_____

_____

_____

_____

_____

2. Do you have any reaction to the inventory Log? _____

_____

_____

_____

_____

_____

_____

_____

_____

_____

3. List specific experiences of taking personal inventory and, when wrong, promptly admitting it. _____

_____

_____

_____

_____

_____

_____

_____

_____

ALLOCATE EQUAL TIME FOR EACH FAMILY MEMBER. PLEASE LIMIT INDIVIDUAL SHARING TO WHAT WAS WRITTEN. ALLOW TIME FOR FEEDBACK FROM FAMILY MEMBERS AFTER WRITING HAS BEEN SHARED.

STEP TEN
PROCESSES AND QUESTIONS FOR WEEK #19 (Step #10 - Week #2)

Continued to take personal inventory and, when we were wrong, promptly admitted it.

1. Review today's thoughts, words, and actions. Describe incidents in which you expressed the following:

    A. Selfishness _____
    _____
    _____

    B. Dishonesty _____
    _____
    _____

    C. Anger_____
    _____
    _____

    D. Fear _____
    _____
    _____
    _____

2. Review today's thoughts, words, and actions. Describe incidents in which you expressed the following:

    A. Generosity _____
    _____
    _____

    B. Honesty_____
    _____
    _____

    C. Calm _____
    _____
    _____

    D. Courage _____
    _____
    _____
    _____

ALLOCATE EQUAL TIME FOR EACH FAMILY MEMBER. PLEASE LIMIT INDIVIDUAL SHARING TO WHAT WAS WRITTEN. ALLOW TIME FOR FEEDBACK FROM FAMILY MEMBERS AFTER WRITING HAS BEEN SHARED.

STEP ELEVEN
PROCESSES AND QUESTIONS FOR WEEK #20 (Step #11 - Week #1)

Sought through prayer and meditation to improve our conscious contact
with God as we understood Him, praying only for knowledge
of His will for us and for the power to carry that out.

1. What thoughts still persist that cause you to stay focused on "your will" when praying for God's guidance? _____

    _____

    _____

    _____

    _____

    _____

    _____

    _____

    _____

    _____

    _____

    _____

    _____

2. What methods of prayer and meditation have you found most useful to you? _____

    _____

    _____

    _____

    _____

    _____

    _____

    _____

    _____

    _____

    _____

    _____

    _____

    _____

    _____

ALLOCATE EQUAL TIME FOR EACH FAMILY MEMBER. PLEASE LIMIT
INDIVIDUAL SHARING TO WHAT WAS WRITTEN. ALLOW TIME FOR FEEDBACK
FROM FAMILY MEMBERS AFTER WRITING HAS BEEN SHARED.

STEP ELEVEN
PROCESSES AND QUESTIONS FOR WEEK #21 (Step #11 - Week #2)

Sought through prayer and meditation to improve our conscious contact
with God as we understood Him, praying only for knowledge
of His will for us and for the power to carry that out.

1. List specific examples of your doing "only God's will." How did you feel?_____

   _____

   _____

   _____

   _____

   _____

   _____

   _____

   _____

   _____

   _____

   _____

2. List specific examples of your "having the courage" to carry out God's will. What
   was the outcome? _____

   _____

   _____

   _____

   _____

   _____

   _____

   _____

   _____

   _____

   _____

   _____

   _____

ALLOCATE EQUAL TIME FOR EACH FAMILY MEMBER. PLEASE LIMIT
INDIVIDUAL SHARING TO WHAT WAS WRITTEN. ALLOW TIME FOR FEEDBACK
FROM FAMILY MEMBERS AFTER WRITING HAS BEEN SHARED.

STEP TWELVE
PROCESSES AND QUESTIONS FOR WEEK #22 (Step #12 - Week #1)

Having had a spiritual awakening as a result of these steps, we tried to carry
this message to others, and to practice these principles in all our affairs.

1. What do you see as the ongoing value of applying the Twelve Steps on a daily basis?

    _____
    _____
    _____
    _____
    _____
    _____
    _____
    _____
    _____
    _____
    _____
    _____
    _____
    _____

2. In what way did the *TWELVE STEP EXERCISE* empower you to more effectively
    handle a life situation? What breakthrough did you experience in having an unexpected
    solution show up?_____

    _____
    _____
    _____
    _____
    _____
    _____
    _____
    _____
    _____
    _____
    _____
    _____
    _____

ALLOCATE EQUAL TIME FOR EACH FAMILY MEMBER. PLEASE LIMIT
INDIVIDUAL SHARING TO WHAT WAS WRITTEN. ALLOW TIME FOR FEEDBACK
FROM FAMILY MEMBERS AFTER WRITING HAS BEEN SHARED.

STEP TWELVE
PROCESSES AND QUESTIONS FOR WEEK #23 (Step #12 - Week #2)

Having had a spiritual awakening as a result of these steps, we tried to carry
this message to others, and to practice these principles in all our affairs.

This is the final Step Study writing exercise. It is an opportunity for you to acknowledge yourself for having the courage to stay and work with other committed people who are seeking a healthier way of life.

1.   Complete the following statements as you now view your life:
     A.   When I was a child, I _____
     _____
     _____

     B.   As I grew into adulthood, I _____
     _____
     _____

     C.   When I became aware of my ACA behavior traits, I_____
     _____
     _____

     D.   Having completed the Step Study, I _____
     _____
     _____

As we may see our life right now, we are the pens through which the ink of our Higher Power flows to write the story of our life. Our Step work and family group have contributed to the deepening of our contact with God. The sharing of each other's experience, strength, and hope has enabled us to expand our faith in our Higher Power and experience unconditional love.

2.   What do you want to say to your family members or to the other individuals of the Step Study relative to:
     A.   Your spiritual awakening: _____
     _____
     _____

     B.   Your gratitude for their coaching you: _____
     _____
     _____

     C.   Your commitment to continue working the Steps: _____
     _____
     _____

ALLOCATE EQUAL TIME FOR EACH FAMILY MEMBER. PLEASE LIMIT INDIVIDUAL SHARING TO WHAT WAS WRITTEN. ALLOW TIME FOR FEEDBACK FROM FAMILY MEMBERS AFTER WRITING HAS BEEN SHARED.

APPENDIX FOUR

SUGGESTED READING

Black, Claudia. *It Will Never Happen To Me*. Denver, CO: Medical Administration Company, 1982.

Cermak, Timmen. *A Primer on Adult Children of Alcoholics*. Pompano Beach, FL: Health Communications, Inc.

Friends in Recovery. *The 12 Steps for Adult Children*. San Diego, CA: Recovery Publications.

Gravitz, H.L., and J.D. Bowden. *Guide to Recovery*. Holmes Beach, FL: Learning Publications, Inc.

Kritsberg, Wayne. *The Adult Children of Alcoholics Syndrome*. Pompano Beach, FL: Health Communications, Inc.

Wegscheider-Cruse, Sharon. *Choicemaking*. Pompano Beach, FL: Health Communications, Inc.

Whitfield, Charles. *Healing the Child Within*. Pompano Beach, FL: Health Communications, Inc.

ORDER FORM

CODE	TITLE	QTY	UNIT PRICE	TOTAL
1058	It Will Never Happen To Me	_____	$ 8.95	_____
1035	A Primer on Adult Children of Alcoholics	_____	$ 3.00	_____
2002	The 12 Steps for Adult Children	_____	$ 6.95	_____
1057	Guide to Recovery	_____	$ 9.95	_____
1034	The Adult Children of Alcoholics Syndrome	_____	$ 7.95	_____
1033	Choicemaking	_____	$ 9.95	_____
1029	Healing the Child Within	_____	$ 8.95	_____
			Sub-Total	_____
			* Sales Tax	_____
		** Shipping & Handling		_____
			TOTAL	_____

Send this order form and a check or money order for the total to:

TOOLS FOR RECOVERY
1201 Knoxville Street
San Diego, CA 92110

To order by phone, please call
(619) 275-1350

* 6% Sales Tax - CA Residents only
** Shpg. & Hand. Min. Charge — $1.75
Orders over $25.00 — $3.00
Orders over $50.00 — 6% of Total

SHIP TO:

Name: _____

Address: _____

City, State: _____

Zip: _____ Phone: (_____)_____

Visa and Mastercard Accepted

Bankcard # _____

Expiration Date _____

Signature _____

Allow 2-3 Weeks for Delivery - UPS

APPENDIX FIVE

THE TWELVE STEPS
OF
ALCOHOLICS ANONYMOUS

1. We admitted we were powerless over alcohol—that our lives had become unmanageable.

2. Came to believe that a Power greater than ourselves could restore us to sanity.

3. Made a decision to turn our will and our lives over to the care of God as we understood Him.

4. Made a searching and fearless moral inventory of ourselves.

5. Admitted to God, to ourselves, and to another human being the exact nature of our wrongs.

6. Were entirely ready to have God remove all these defects of character.

7. Humbly asked Him to remove our shortcomings.

8. Made a list of all persons we had harmed, and became willing to make amends to them all.

9. Made direct amends to such people wherever possible, except when to do so would injure them or others.

10 Continued to take personal inventory and when we were wrong promptly admitted it.

11. Sought through prayer and meditation to improve our conscious contact with God as we understood Him, praying only for knowledge of His will for us and the power to carry that out.

12. Having had a spiritual awakening as the result of these steps, we tried to carry this message to alcoholics, and to practice these principles in all our affairs.

Reprinted with permission of
ALCOHOLICS ANONYMOUS
WORLD SERVICES, INC.